D1395501

Aberdeenshire Library and Information Service
www.aberdeenshire.gov.uk/libraries
Renewals Hotline 01224 661511

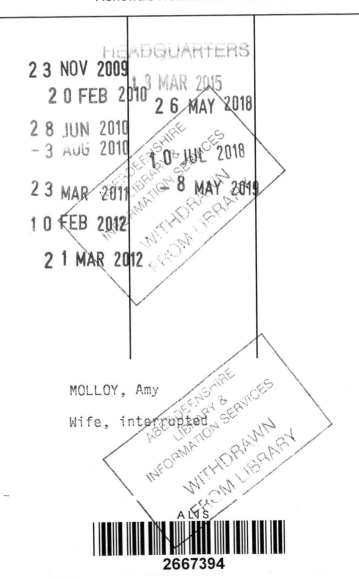

MOLLOY, Amy

Wife, interrupted

Wife, Interrupted

Wife, Interrupted

Amy Molloy

headline
review

First published in 2009
by HEADLINE REVIEW

An imprint of HEADLINE PUBLISHING GROUP

1

Cataloguing in Publication Data is available from the British Library

Hardback ISBN 978 0 7553 1954 1
Trade paperback ISBN 978 0 7553 1955 8

Typeset in Garamond MT by Palimpsest Book Production Limited,
Grangemouth, Stirlingshire

Printed and bound in Great Britain by
Clays Ltd, St Ives plc

Headline's policy is to use papers that are natural, renewable and recyclable
products and made from wood grown in sustainable forests. The logging
and manufacturing processes are expected to conform to the
environmental regulations of the country of origin.

For my parents –

who've always supported me
even when they haven't agreed with me.

And of course Eoghan –

who gave me a story to tell.

I love you all.

The names of some of the people and places, as well as some physical descriptions have been changed to protect the privacy of the individuals concerned.

Introduction

August 2009

By the time my husband had been dead thirteen months, I had slept with twenty-seven men. Because sex I can do: at sex I'm a pro. Whether right or wrong, I was having sex just three months after he died; slipping back into a pubescent autopilot; gasping in the appropriate places and going down obediently when required. And it may not have been good sex, but it was safe sex. Not in the gynaecological sense, but in the sense that I was detached: void of emotion, void of a history and completely anonymous. To whichever man shared my bed that evening I was nothing more than a female anatomy. And that was just fine with me. Because at twenty-three years old, with one dead husband under my belt and a widow's shroud around my shoulders, anonymous was a tonic: anonymous was just perfect.

I won't go into the details of my husband's death right now – it will just make you feel uncomfortable – just as you won't hear about all the men I've been with since, only the important ones – but, needless to say, I was married once: over two years ago. I was a wife for exactly thirty-two days before my wonderful husband passed away, late one Monday evening. The cause of death was cancer, which started as malignant melanoma, and a mole on his chest he had had removed two years before, but quickly and silently spread to his liver, lungs, pancreas and, finally, his brain. It was this tumour that led to the stroke.

Yes, we were told it was terminal, but I can tell you that nothing prepares you. We were convinced we could prove the doctors wrong.

My husband's name was Eoghan, and he was an Irishman, with the usual charm and more. I lived in Dublin for the duration of his treatment, so he could be near his family: his mother and three brothers. I'll tell you he was thirty-six when he died, but that's enough detail for now. In twelve months of chemotherapy everything focused on him. Now, I want the attention back on me. I've forgotten how that feels.

My promiscuous reaction to Eoghan's death surprised everyone, none more so than me. There is a certain way a widow, of any age, is expected to behave, and sleeping around is usually frowned upon. But let me get this straight right now, before you're tempted to judge me: I loved – love – my husband. I was a loyal wife and a devoted carer, and if his body could have lived with the cancer, I'd have nursed him for a lifetime, just happy to be with him. To watch him die was indescribable.

My beautiful, beautiful husband was, to me, simply perfect. When we first met, and began sharing a bed, I'd lie awake for hours just taking him in. I had every inch of his face committed to memory: the contours of his skin, each lash that traced his eyelids.

In that final hour, as he lay swaddled in a hospital bed, I barely recognized him. His lips were purple, his skin had yellowed. Even his odour was that of a stranger. I pressed my cheek against his chest, measuring its rise and fall. The gap between each gasp was lengthening. I wanted it to be over for him. I wanted him to be free. I pressed my lips close to his ear, so neither his family nor the doctors could hear me and I whispered: 'You can go now, Eoghan. Please go now. And know you haven't let me down. We did everything we could, my baby. You did everything you promised me you would. Now it's time for you to leave me.'

As I stopped speaking, he stopped breathing.

So you see, it's not that I didn't love my husband. My behaviour since has no bearing on my love for him. I said my wedding vows with utter conviction. For better, for worse, for richer, for poorer, in sickness and in health: that part was nice and easy. The Catholic church maps out the 'do's and don't's quite clearly. But, I ask, what comes after the death us do part?

Initially, after Eoghan died, I was sure I'd never be with another man. But it's one of life's great mysteries that you can't predict how you react to a tragedy, as since then my actions have been the absolute opposite of my intentions. So don't read any further if you want a widow on a pedestal; don't bother with chapter two if you're hoping for a heroine. My story isn't sinless, but I promise you it's honest. That's all I wanted it to be.

Looking back on my final year with Eoghan, I'm not quite sure how, logistically, I juggled my responsibilities. In the last legs of his – failing – chemotherapy I cared for him, studied for the final exams of my journalism degree and worked part-time for a fashion magazine. I'd fly from Dublin to Heathrow and then drive an hour to my university in Southampton once a week for lectures – though these trips became less and less frequent as Eoghan got sicker and I couldn't bear to leave him. Just in case that day might be 'the' day.

God knows how I did it, but I did it somehow, and two weeks after Eoghan died I got my university results, passing with a 2:1. Three months after Eoghan died I came back to England, moved home with my parents and became an intern at a fashion magazine. Life goes on, whether you want it to or not, though you might not be ready for it.

When Eoghan first died I thought, I can do this, this isn't so bad. I figured I must be unusually strong, untouchable even, because I could still function, walk, talk, and go on as normal. I didn't see it was merely adrenaline that was keeping me going, and that my 'normal' behaviour was far from it. I coped quite well until after the funeral, as I focused on the tasks at hand – picking hymns, meeting and greeting relatives, collecting his last belongings from the hospital – but when the funeral was over, the guests had gone home and the party food and flowers had been relegated to the dustbin, I realized I had nothing to live for any more. That's when the pain gave way to numbness, and an invisibility cloak was pulled over my head. I stopped thinking about Eoghan, or about the past. I had no interest in the present and, honestly, hoped I wouldn't have a future. I was unreachable.

Then, whilst mindlessly surfing the internet one day, I saw an advert searching for a flatmate for a house share in

London, and found myself replying. Four weeks later, I moved in with three girls who, without exaggeration, became my salvation.

We have a pact never to mention 'dead husband' in the presence of an attractive male – I learned very early that mortality isn't a turn-on – and when I emerge from my bedroom on the morning after the night before, back covered in scratches, a bite mark in the crook of my neck and a request for cranberry juice to cure my honeymoon cystitis, they never judge me. They understand we all do what it takes to get by.

We joke I have a fetish for threesomes. As the front door slams behind my conquest's back, the girls and I laugh at his obliviousness. Little did he know that, as he slept smugly, as he spooned this nameless, naked blonde in one-night-only intimacy, her dead husband's spirit was tucked in bed beside them. But I sometimes think the last laugh's on me, because three is a crowd and I don't know how to find room in my heart for him and them.

Because, believe me, Eoghan never leaves. He is the steadying constant in my life, and has been since the day he first kissed me, and I'm sure as hell not trying to replace him.

This other temporary bed partner is just a hapless bystander: a means of physical tactility whilst my husband is temporarily engaged, elsewhere.

I don't do it because my sex drive's high, or for the notches on my bedpost. It's hardly about pleasure. I couldn't care less if I orgasm. Yet night after night, for twelve months after Eoghan's death, I chased men to share my bed, and why? I did it for the ones who'd plant a kiss on the tip of my nose once they'd come. And the men who stroked my hair, just as Eoghan used to do when I was scared. And the ones who said I was beautiful, as they turned and walked out the door. I did it for those moments that reminded me what it was like to be worth something. I did it because the rest of the time I ached with loneliness. I did it to feel normal again, or at least to feel something.

Chapter One

As made crystal clear, I have no qualms about sharing my bed with a stranger. However, I should clarify that I'm not available to just anyone: the aesthetic appeal of said bed-hopper must be of a standard, must meet certain requirements. Eoghan was a surfer: a long-haired vagabond with obtrusive tattoos and a face-splitting smile. Now, more out of habit than conscious decision, I veer towards a similar style. This rules out suits, toffs and trustafarians. On the other hand, if you're a scuffed-up outdoorsy type with a questionable background, it's your lucky night.

I can't remember the name of the first man I slept with after Eoghan. It was twelve weeks after he died, and now, looking back, I see that this was such a short amount of time. An old university friend had convinced me to go on a night out in Southampton, where I'd studied for my degree.

Shona hadn't seen me for two years. Although we'd met on our first day, during fresher's week, I'd since taken a year out to go travelling, so in the end she'd graduated a year before me. We'd kept in touch through polite emails and text messages, but had naturally grown more and more distant with the demands of grown-up life. She became a pole dancer in a local strip joint – which just shows you what four years of university and £30,000 of student debt gets you – and I had taken a much different path. She'd heard about Eoghan's death, of course, and the fact that I'd since come back to England to live with my parents, and had texted me to say: 'You need cheering up. Come to a foam party in Southampton – it'll be just like old times.' I thought, Jesus, that's not me any more. I hadn't drunk alcohol in almost a year, since Eoghan was first diagnosed, and hadn't been clubbing in God knows how long. I was a wife and carer and, even with Eoghan dead and buried, I still hadn't broken free of this role. I had responsibilities. I couldn't go swanning off to bars. I couldn't have *fun*. I spat out the word in disgust. In my mouth it tasted bitter. My husband was dead – had everyone forgotten already?

I'm not sure what changed my mind and made me go to meet her. Possibly the thought of spending another weekend with my parents tutting and fussing and looking at me despairingly. Partly it was intrigue. I wanted to see how my old friends now lived, the life I could have had if I hadn't met Eoghan and been thrown into all this.

So I borrow my Mum's car and drive the hour to Southampton, thinking I can feign illness and drive home if it all gets too much. I bring one bottle of white wine with me. I think, maybe I can have a small glass, just to loosen myself up before we go out. After that, though, I'll only drink water. Or Coke. But there's a lot of sugar in Coke. No, no, I'll stick to water, I decide.

I stand on Shona's doorstep and ring the bell with a

shaking hand. The door is flung open, and there she is, exactly the same as I remember – dressed up in a mini skirt and skyscraper heels. Wearing the same plastic charm bracelet we both bought in a market and wore religiously though our second year at university. How could one person's life stay so still?

'Amy,' she cries, sweeping me into a bearhug. 'Come in, we've just got the drinking rolling.' I notice an empty tequila glass in her hand, remnants of salt pixillating its rim.

She doesn't wait for a reply but takes me by the hand and pulls me up a dark staircase, from the top of which comes the sound of chaos: laughter, house music, the clash of bottles. I'm fucking terrified.

Then I think of Eoghan. I remember him on our wedding day – leading a conga around the hotel's reception room, determined to make the most of his day, but clenching his teeth when the pain came in waves. It's sink or swim, Amy, I think: you can still be that girl, the fresher Shona remembers. And I desperately want to be that girl again. Back then I had so little to be frightened of.

As we reach the top of the staircase I find my voice: 'It's wicked to see you, Sho,' I holler over the music. 'I've got some cheap vino. Thought we could mix it with vodka. Just like old times.'

We're at the bar. I am drunk. Very drunk. One bottle of wine, six vodkas and four shots of Sambuca sort of drunk. I don't know where Shona is right now. She was last seen pressed against the bar, with her tongue down some poor boy's throat.

I'm in the centre of the dance floor, surrounded by people, pressed body to body and nose to nose. The heat of those people, their energy, seeps into my skin. It recharges me, it awakens me. And the noise – my head, my whole body vibrates with the beat of the music. I'm dancing: my arms are held above my head as my arse sways from side to side, bouncing rhythmically against the hips of the person next to me. I'm not conscious of moving my body – it dances of its own accord, as if it's been waiting to do this for a long time.

Foam rains down – sticky, acidic bubbles of chemical – which, to me, looks like the most beautiful snowfall. I spin around, my face raised to the ceiling, and laugh for what feels like the first time since Eoghan died. I'm alive.

Someone grabs my waist though the foam. Large hands, men's hands. I reach out and touch his face through the bubbles, but as quickly as I wipe it away it rains down and camouflages him again. The grip on my waist gets firmer and he pulls me towards him, his groin pressed against my stomach. Then he kisses me. And it is better that I can't see his face. It's easier to cope with somehow. I try to convince myself: I can pretend this is my husband.

But I'd forgotten what it's like to kiss a stranger. When you kiss someone you love, it's soft and intimate. Kiss a stranger, and it's rough, raw, it's all about sex and nothing more. There's nothing quite like it, and there's no way I can kid myself that this is Eoghan. No, this is quite different.

His hands are on my arse now, fingers creeping under the hem of my skirt, digging into the flesh of my thigh. He bites my lip and the metallic taste of blood cuts across my tongue. He sees me. He actually wants me. When for so many months I've felt invisible. I break away from the kiss. 'Come home with me tonight,' I whisper in his ear – testing the new phrase out for size. I like it. I'm in control, I'm powerful, alive: 'Come home with me.'

He comes back to Shona's house with me; we fuck, though my memory of this is hazy, then fall asleep with our legs and arms intertwined. The next morning my hangover numbs the guilt. He leaves before I wake, which is perfectly fine with me: he was no more than a prop in this experiment anyway. On the hour-long drive back to Buckinghamshire, I can't help but stare at myself in the rear-view mirror. I look different somehow, revived. Since Eoghan's death my complexion has been almost transparently pale, but today I have a rosy tint to the apples of my cheeks. My mouth is swollen, with a red mark across my lower lip where he bit into it. It stings when I touch it, so I touch it repeatedly, enjoying the bittersweet pain.

I pull into the drive of my parents' house, where they're sitting in the living room, waiting for me. I throw my overnight bag in the hallway and stroll in with my chest puffed out and chin held high.

'Did you have a good night?' my darling daddy asks anxiously.

'Yes I did,' I reply. 'We went to a bar, we danced. I had a one-night stand.'

I stare him in the eye, not blinking, willing him to challenge me. High on the adrenaline of last night, I'm ready for a fight, for the release of raised voices, and uncensored words; for them to do anything but mollycoddle me.

But my poor father, so full of love for his younger daughter, holds his tongue, and says nothing. Seconds pass.

Nobody is sure of the correct response. None of us has stood here before.

In the end my mum breaks the silence: 'Why don't you go and have a bath?' she says. 'I'll bring you up a cup of tea and a digestive.'

I draw a sharp, deep breath in, and as I breathe out, my new-found energy drains out of me, and I deflate back into the withered shape of the wounded and dejected: my shoulders slump, my eye line falls to the floor, and I feel a veil of grief fall across my face once more. Why can't they criticize me, argue with me, tell me I'm wrong? Why can't they hate me like they should for disrespecting their beloved son-in-law's memory?

Go on, Mother, I think, tell me I'm a whore, a cheap bit of tart. You never held back before Eoghan died, you were my harshest and most valued critic. Don't hold back on me now. Call me a slut. Give me an excuse to scream and yell and shout right back.

But, of course, she won't. Because nobody wants to upset the widow. And I wonder if things will ever be normal again.

I lie in the bath, run for me by my mum, and sip the super-sweet tea she has brought up to me. Before Eoghan, when the closest I'd come to bereavement was the death of an aged grandparent, I never knew grief could change you in so many ways. There's the tears and the anger, the fear; that's a given. I'd watched enough soap operas to expect those side effects. But no one warns you that, physically, you'll never quite feel the same as you did before you watched that coffin lower.

For one, my eyes are permanently blurred; like looking

at life through a greyish tint. And my legs feel as if they're made of lead, the effort of walking so great that sometimes I just don't bother, and sit for days, almost motionless, instead. And my sense of taste is shot to bits. Like a pregnant woman, I gag at the stench of certain foods: frying omelettes, mashed potatoes, and most smells that remind me of the meals they serve in hospitals. My periods have stopped completely – my last menstrual bleed was on the day of Eoghan's funeral – and, bizarrely enough, my fingernails have stopped growing. It's like my body no longer responds to me.

I lift my right foot from the bathwater and press it against the boiling metal of the hot-water tap. I know this should hurt, so why can't I feel it? A flush of red spreads across my foot, from where the tap burns into the skin, yet still I feel nothing. I think back to last night and am actually disappointed I don't feel guilty. Guilt, even regret, would be more satisfying than this nothingness. That just proves how much I've changed.

Before Eoghan, I was no saint, but no different to any other girl of a certain age. I've always been an outrageous flirt, but my sex life was generally quite innocent. I was stubbornly single through one year at art college and two years at university and, though I kissed many men, I bedded very few, preferring to wake up alone of a weekend, so I could go for an early-morning swim or head to the library. Naturally, I had the odd one-night stand, but it really wasn't my thing. I didn't need it back then.

Eoghan was the first boyfriend I'd had in two years, and the first man I'd slept with regularly and with such intimacy. Before him there were a couple of teenage romances, but neither would qualify as a real relationship, and the sex was young and naive: experimental, but not always successful – you know the kind.

At university, that handful of one-night stands taught me some tricks, and over the first six months of my travels I slept with a further three guys, but, as one gentleman told me whilst re-buttoning his jeans and high-fiving his mate on the bunk bed above us: 'This is all part of the backpacking experience.'

When I met Eoghan in Byron Bay, midway through a gap year I'd taken after my second year at university, the last thing on my mind was settling down. On this trip I wanted no worries, responsibilities or emotional attachments. That's exactly what I was running from.

About a year before I went to Australia, the summer between my first and second year at university, my father, a man I hero-worship, according to my mother, was diagnosed with cancer: Stage IV Hodgkin's Lymphoma. For those of you not in the know, Stage IV in the case of lymphoma means the cancer has spread from its primary source to more than one other organ. In other words, it has not been caught early.

I sat with my father through every chemo session, and every blood test that told us the chemo was failing, but as the odds of him surviving plummeted, I began to fracture, mentally. Each day he seemed to age five years, and as I watched him grow thinner and thinner, I knew I couldn't be there if and when the end came. So I ran away, booking a flight to Australia, with my parents' love and blessing – they said they were happy to have one less person to worry about.

I knew I was fragile and that the easiest thing would be to find a man, a father figure, to take care of me. But I knew, deep down, this wouldn't answer my problems. I needed to find the strength in me again, or else, when I returned to England, as I had to do at some point, I'd be back to square one. So, as my plane flew into Sydney, I made a pact to be on my own. I wouldn't rely on anyone – especially a man – to look after me or make my adventure a fulfilling one.

As it turns out, Eoghan had other ideas. According to him – and you'll have to take my word for this – the first night he saw me he knew he would marry me, and he turned to his friend Nigel and told him so. Nigel would tell me at the funeral how shocked he was at this declaration – coming from Eoghan, a confirmed bachelor who had told all his friends he had no intention to marry, but that he, Nigel, had instantly believed him.

Eoghan and I were so different on paper, and when we started dating everyone around us said we'd never last the summer.

He was thirty-four when we met in Byron Bay, whilst I was just twenty-one: my twenty-second birthday was still a few months away. I would have gasped at a thirteen-year age gap before, but if you'd known Eoghan you'd understand why it was irrelevant. Eoghan had a unique, ageless quality about him: he could blend into any social group, mix in with children, parents or grandparents and instantly be accepted into their midst. He was a unique contradiction: with a youthful sense of humour, energy and optimism, yet the wisdom and compassion of someone way beyond his years.

Looks-wise, well, handsome doesn't cut it. He was truly beautiful – he'd hate me saying that, but a more masculine adjective just isn't fitting – with eyes that were in between blue, green and grey and an infectious smile you couldn't help but copy. I fell for him hard, from the height of a skyscraper, and though it took me a while to step over the edge, when I did he gently cushioned my landing.

I was so fragile then, and elusively guarded. I'd been in Oz almost half a year, and nobody knew about my sick father, back in England. When they asked about family, I omitted that detail. When they asked why I was crying, I said premenstrual tension. I preferred it that way. I needed that distance. So, when I had to call home, I'd walk two miles down the beach, to where the tide was riskier, so there were less surfers and swimmers, and I could talk in peace, dry my eyes and then return to my friends with an unbroken smile.

'How are you, Daddy?'

'I'm fine, pet, doing well.'

'How are you, Amy?'

'I'm fine, Daddy, having a great time.'

To this day, the F-word turns my stomach. Because 'Fine' is a euphemism for everything you're scared of saying. 'Fine' means: 'My treatment's failed and I'm getting my affairs in order.' 'Fine' means: 'I'm scared that by the time I fly home you'll be dead.'

So I told nobody about my father's illness, learned to contort my history, censor conversations and dodge any uncomfortably personal questions. It wasn't hard, as travellers don't tend to pry: many have their own secrets to hide. Eoghan, I found out later, was no exception:

running from a well-hidden cocaine habit that had cost him hundreds a week and caused him to roll his car into a ditch. He'd left Dublin to escape this destructive cycle, and had, to give him his due, given up class As, but since replaced the object of his addiction with alcohol.

Hence why, when I met Eoghan, in Byron Bay, in the lead-up to Christmas 2005, he was pissed as a fart. Not just on one occasion, but every time I met him, without exception. Now I'm not teetotal – far from it. Many of the stories you'll hear forthwith end at the bottom of a vodka bottle, but Eoghan, well, he was in another league entirely. He was a messy drunk, always falling and drooling, and could easily stomach two bottles of wine and a bottle of vodka, on his own, in one evening. He would later admit to me he was verging on alcoholism – a fact that was obvious a mile off.

The problem was that he was undoubtedly terrific fun to party with. He was infamous in the area as the local Jack the lad: boisterous and flirtatious, he never stood still and never appeared to quite sober up, but he was the man everyone wanted to be friends with. With Eoghan in residence, at least you would never have a mundane night.

I, on the other hand, was a barmaid at the corniest back-packer bar in town, where the regulation uniform was a bikini, sometimes bizarrely matched with a policewoman's hat, and flirting was part of the job description. You can't work in a place like that without adopting a certain 'tartish' reputation, but in fact mine was largely unfounded as, though I kissed many admirers, I rarely went further, and it was unheard of for me to take home a punter. That said, in a small town such as Byron Bay, plenty of rumours did the rounds and I know Eoghan heard a few tasty titbits about me, including a whisper that I was sleeping with my manager. I know this one was spread by the girls I worked with, who were pissed off that I seemed to be given the best shifts on the rota. I wasn't (sleeping with him), just so you know. The manager in question was actually having an affair with my best friend, and as I was the only other employee who knew, he gave me those shifts in return for my silence.

Anyway, none of these stories seemed to bother Eoghan, or else he was too drunk to remember them by morning as, one night, in his customary position, propping up the beer taps, he beckoned me over, leant across the bar and whispered: 'Amy, you're the most beautiful girl in Byron Bay. You're the most beautiful girl I've ever seen. If you were my girlfriend I'd treat you like a princess every day.'

It would have been hard for him to hear my response over the bellowed drinks requests from those around him, but he must have caught the gist. 'Fuck off, Eoghan, don't you realize? No girl wants to date a drunk,' I spat back.

It's not quite the fairy-tale start you'd imagine for two strangers who were engaged nine weeks later. And, sadly, I can take no credit for the fact that true love did win out. I was stubbornly bull-headed, with low expectations, and had no faith he'd remember what he said the next day, let alone my stinging retort.

But he did. And what's more he returned the next night, and six more after that, each time repeating the promise, word perfect: 'If you were my girlfriend I'd treat you like a princess every day,' he would say, then before I had a chance to reply he'd turn on his heels and disappear into the crowd.

He also gave up alcohol. I didn't notice at first, but then night after night he'd come into the bar and nurse a glass of lemonade, to much ribbing from his friends. He even gave up cigarettes – another habit he knew I hated – and instead I'd spot him chewing on cocktail sticks soaked in tea-tree oil, oblivious to the stares and jokes at his expense. He may have noticed and simply didn't care. The smell of tea tree still takes me straight back to our early dates, when he would jam the sticks in his buttonholes whilst he sucked on a fruit smoothie, and twirl them in his fingertips whilst we walked along the sea edge.

Eoghan intrigued me. He'd told me he thought I was beautiful, so I knew he was attracted to me, but why then did he never try to kiss me? Unlike the usual backpacker boys, who would grab your arse, lift your skirt or stick their tongue in your ear without asking, Eoghan just watched from the sidelines: always there, but never intimidating. He'd stay in the bar until the end of my shift, simply kiss me on the cheek, and bid me goodnight, but then the next morning would knock on my door on the dot of seven, to ask if I'd like to go surfing, or to drop in a punnet of strawberries or a bag of warm muffins for my roommates and me to have for our breakfast.

I'd come home from a day spent at the beach to find him napping in the hammock strung from the wooden front porch of my house, seemingly careless and content to wait indefinitely. Time never seemed important to him, he didn't rush or hurry for anyone, and having been brought up in cities all my life, I'd never met anyone quite like him. Although I was still adamant I didn't want a boyfriend, I found myself missing him on the days I didn't see him.

It was New Year's Eve before Eoghan actually kissed me. He'd invited me to a party – this wasn't significant, as he'd also invited most of the town – in the garden of the surf school where he lived and worked. The grass and concrete yard were swarming with guests, partygoers sat on the roofs of wooden sheds where the surfboards were stored, and in the branches of trees that bordered the property. A makeshift DJ booth had been set up on top of a tall iron crate, where the club's trailer was kept, and braver guests had climbed a precarious-looking ladder to sit on its top, sandwiched between vibrating speakers, and cupping their mouths to be heard over the blast.

I was dancing in the centre of the courtyard, which was heaving. Person to person and flesh to flesh, my shoulders bounced off those of my neighbours, and it was impossible to see past the person in front of you. I stood on my tiptoes to peer over the crowd: I hadn't seen Eoghan since he greeted me with a kiss on the cheek, and a Jim Beam and Coke, as I arrived. Then I see him weaving towards me, his blond hair damp and swept across his forehead in an angel's curl.

'Amox,' he bellows over the bassline. 'Come dance with me, I'm missing you.'

He reaches out for my hand, and as I slip mine into his, I feel something round, cool and hard being pressed into my palm. I glance up and he winks. 'A New Year's present,' he says.

I open my fist and the spotlight from the clubhouse hits the gift and makes it shine. It's a piece of stone, with a pale-pink hue, perfectly smooth, and small enough to nestle, neatly, between the heart and head lines in my palm.

'What is it?' I ask him.

'It's rose quartz,' he replies, placing his hand over mine to cup the perfect stone inside. 'It's the gemstone of the heart. I have a piece too. See.' He reaches into his pocket and pulls out an almost identical stone, only slightly larger, and rougher around the edges than my own.

'See, I'll carry my piece and, hopefully, you'll carry yours.' He blushes, so deeply I can see it through the darkness. I've never seen Eoghan look flustered before. 'And it will help you let yourself love me. It will help you to trust me. You're an odd one, Amy: you're so friendly and bubbly, but there's a part of you held back. I don't know what you're scared of, but believe me when I say I won't let anything hurt you. I want to take care of you.'

I clasp my fingers over the stone, and it pulses like a heart in my palm. Today, Eoghan is buried with his piece of quartz, whilst mine lies in the depths of my underwear drawer. I used to carry it everywhere with me, but as the months passed after Eoghan's death the heartbeat grew slower and then stopped altogether. Now, when I pick it up, it's just a run-of-the-mill garden rock. But, back then, when Eoghan gave it to me, it meant everything. And when I accepted it, he knew I was accepting him.

It's one minute to midnight and a countdown begins, numbers yelled in unison from sixty to one. Eoghan grabs my hand.

'Come with me,' he shouts above the din, pushing

through the crowd to the DJ's station and stepping on to the bottom rung of the ladder.

'Oh God,' I groan, glancing at the crate, which is shuddering with the music's bass.

'You'll be fine with me,' he says firmly. 'That's what I've been trying to say all this time. You'll always be safe with me, Ame.'

He pulls me towards the ladder, grips my hands around the rungs, and we climb up together, me slightly in front, his arms like banisters on either side of me.

When we reach the top, he spins me round.

'Worth it, huh?' he asks.

Below us is a sea of faces, gleaming, turned up to the sky, some shouting and some singing, some waving sparklers or metallic gold streamers. Their energy rises up like a cloud and engulfs us. It wraps me up and cradles me.

Then Eoghan turns me round and kisses me, and his arms around my waist, combined with the force from the crowd, forms a steel cage that I know no danger can ever penetrate. I take a step back and my heel slips over the edge of the crate, but Eoghan's arms around my waist hold me in place. At last I'm safe.

The celebrations go on until three o'clock the next afternoon. As the last guests say their goodbyes to make for their beds, Eoghan says: 'Do you fancy walking up to the lighthouse?'

'Yes, I'd love to.' I'm utterly exhausted, shivering with tiredness, and the lighthouse is a three-mile walk uphill, but right then, I'd have followed him anywhere.

We trudge up the hill, hand in hand, to Byron Bay lighthouse: the easternmost point in Australia, where if you look left and right there's no land on either side – for ever.

A cement platform juts out from the cliff, used as a launch pad for paragliders, and it's there we sit, both looking out to sea, me sitting in between his knees.

It's blustery up here, with the on-shore wind in our faces, and I'm thankful for my sweatshirt, the hood pulled up to block my ears from the gusts.

'So, Amy,' he says. 'What exactly are you running from?'

I look around for a bolt-hole. I want to hide. I'll have to lie.

Then I realize he's still talking, and he's telling me his own story: about sour friendships back home, the mistakes he's made, and how scared he feels of going back to that place. He's crying.

I turn on to my knees, to face him: kiss the tears which run down his cheeks and tell him it'll be OK. And then I tell him about myself. I tell him everything. Our tears run and blend and, together, they taste more sweet than salty.

Three weeks later Eoghan proposes, in his atypical fashion: over a plate of beans on toast, as we sit cross-legged in the camper van I'd bought that week, pulling a piece of looped coral from his pocket and offering it as a ring.

'Will you marry me, Amy?' he asks audaciously, raising one eyebrow.

Of course, I say yes – there was no other answer. Life was so simple back then.

With Eoghan, every day was a celebration. He brought the energy and euphoria of that New Year's Eve into our day-to-day lives and sustained it somehow, making each day a new adventure for us. I don't know how he did it:

he simply had a heightened way of living, and I've never met anyone with that ability before or since.

God, I miss that high. Now, my life is one thick-set, straight line.

But what's the point in reminiscing? He's gone now. And I'm left here: lying in a bathtub of greying water, not caring that it's now uncomfortably cool, thinking that things need to change.

In the last few months, I've been showered with praise from family and friends: how wonderful I was with Eoghan, how doting a carer, how brave a mourner. But nobody remembers I'm more than the achievements of the last year. No one, not even me, can remember who I was before.

That man last night didn't know my story. He wanted me for the superficialities: blonde hair, pretty smile, nice arse maybe. He didn't fuck me because he felt sorry for me. He fucked me because he liked what he saw, even if just in the short term.

Even the sting from this cut on my lip is a pleasant distraction, a welcome change from the numbness I've been ensconced in for so long. I emerge from the now lukewarm water of the bathtub and catch a glimpse of myself in the bathroom mirror, admiring a small purple bruise on my arse cheek, a tiny bite mark on my shoulder. It proves I'm still reachable; still human, still someone. Proves that a stranger wanted me enough to reach out and grab me. I smile, empowered; the muscles in my cheeks stretch, aching and yawning. It's been that long since I've smiled and meant it.

Ten days later, the bruise has yellowed, my lip has

scabbed, and the old, familiar numbness has returned. I'm back to the confines of my parents' sofa, cocooned in a blanket, wearing my oldest pyjamas and a jumper of Eoghan's, idly checking my email's overflowing inbox, with no motivation to reply to any of the sympathy emails people are still sending. My mind swims back to that night in Southampton, and how wonderful it was to feel like an average twenty-three-year-old again.

My foot's going to sleep where my legs have been tucked under my bottom too long, so I uncurl myself and, swaddling myself in a blanket like a baby, shuffle towards the kitchen to make a cup of tea. As I reach the glass-panelled kitchen door, which is – unusually for our household – pulled closed, I can see the stooped figures of my mum and dad through it. The door is just slightly ajar, enough for me to hear their hushed conversation, just about.

'But I'm her mother.' My mum's voice sounds cracked and old, though she's only in her forties: 'Surely I should have known the answer. But I don't have a clue what to do. I thought it'd be all right, as soon as she came home from Ireland, that I could protect her, bring her peace of some sort, but there's nothing for her here any more.'

The silhouettes in the window shift, as my dad puts his arm around her to soothe her.

She lets out a sigh, like a wounded animal, and behind the closed door I pull my blanket more tightly around my shoulders.

'Do you know, Steve: I had to dress her this morning? She wouldn't – couldn't – even get out of bed. I had to coax her up and dress her, like when she was a baby: pull her arms through the sleeves of her jumper and brush her hair. Remember that pudgy little six-month-old Amy: always with her arms reaching out to be picked up? It was so uncomplicated then. I could bath her, and dress her in a clean nightie, and tuck her in her cot, guarded and intact. Now I don't know what to do. Here, with us, there's nothing we can do to make this better.'

The words keep flowing, and I wonder how long I can stand here and listen. I feel like I'm intruding, but can't tear myself away, like picking a scab: I can't feel it now, but know in an hour it'll start to sting again.

'There's too much of Eoghan in this house, Steve,' she continues. 'His shoes are in the cupboard under the stairs: his coat's still hanging up next to yours. Every time I open Amy's wardrobe I see her wedding gown. I can't throw these things away, but how can she move forward when there're reminders of him everywhere. She needs to begin again.'

'I know,' my father chides. 'But she'll do it in her own time.'

'But how?' My mother's figure folds, and she clutches the sides of the sink, for support. 'Where does she go from here, what can she do now? I don't know who she can be, without him.'

Hearing my mother echoing my darkest fears and asking the same questions I've been running from, I can't listen any more. Turning my slippered feet, I pad quietly back to the living room, leaving them to wrestle with a conversation I know won't give them any answers.

Mostly out of habit, I numbly reboot my laptop and scroll through the history of my latest internet searches. That's when I spot an advert looking for a housemate.

Why not? I think, because it seems we've all agreed that I can't go on like this.

Six weeks later I move out of my parents' and in with Rachel, Victoria and Lucy. These friendships are fresh, clean and untarnished. They never knew Eoghan and they have no preconceived expectations of me. I don't need to grieve around them. I can be who I want to be. I can be free.

I want to be the girl I caught a glimpse of that one night in Southampton. That girl hadn't been hurt, she wasn't damaged or fragile. That girl could rule the world.

When your heart is broken, however, such a façade is hard to uphold. This is where the men come in handy. They energize me, these one-night stands, like plugging myself into the mains. They come, we have sex: they bolster my confidence. They distract me from my memories – if only for a short time.

Aiden was one of many but is worth mentioning because, unlike the others, he was the first man since Eoghan to get under my skin. We meet in January, six months after Eoghan died, whilst standing, shivering, in line outside a bar in Hoxton Square.

Conforming to the stereotype of a girls' night out, French Martinis have been the drink of the evening, and my housemates and I are a little unsteady. As we take our place at the back of the queue I accidentally dig one five-inch heel into the fleshy toecap of my neighbour's shoe. He swears and spins to face me.

'I'm really sorry,' I chirp insincerely, glancing at his profile and thanking fate for intervening. His hair is dark, shoulder-length and swept into a ponytail. For such a feminine style, there is something deeply masculine about its length.

'That's OK,' he says and turns back to his friend.

At this point many girls would admit defeat, but the desperation of a widow on the pull is insatiable.

I tap him on the shoulder: 'Excuse me.'

'Yes?'

'I was wondering.'

'What?'

'Can I get in your coat?'

Before you ask, even if you had been there, what I said wouldn't have made sense. Not surprisingly, he looks bemused and is no more convinced when I explain that I'm cold and would like to share his jacket for warmth.

With this short interchange I have proven myself insane. The velveteen rope at the entrance to the club signals the end of our enforced time together. Our party of five files through the doors, splits into our own, separate groups, with him vanishing into the revelling crowd. I admit defeat and write him off. Note to self: must engage mouth and brain before speaking. Lesson learned; move on, I thought.

Except Aiden – who, it appeared, was attracted to lunacy – had other ideas. The next thing I know, I bump into him at the bar. And on the dance floor. And outside the toilets. This can't be a coincidence.

When, three hours later, I lose the girls and am left circling the dance floor, searching for a familiar face through vodka-strained eyes, I feel somebody take hold of my hand and guide me into a clearing.

'You look like you could do with rescuing,' Aiden says,

brushing my fringe from my forehead, where it's stuck with sweat to my brow.

'I've lost the girls,' I mumble.

'I'll help you to find them.'

But instead he kisses me.

The kiss is soft and gentle, and his hands cup my cheeks. I entwine my fingers in his hair, pulling strands from the ponytail and watching them unfurl down his neck. I have a mind prone to fantasies, and right now it's pornographic.

'Do you want to come back to mine?' I confidently ask, sure he'll jump at the chance.

'No I don't,' he replies, flooring me. 'But give me your number and I'll call you.'

This sort of behaviour is way outside my comfort zone. One-night stands I can do (place heavy emphasis on the 'one'), but my brief encounters never lead to repeat performances. Plus, the bar we're in is an infamous pick-up joint. People don't come here to find a plus one. They come here to fill themselves with cut-price beer, fondle strangers in darkened corners and leave at 4 a.m. with no strings trailing at their heels. But there is something appealing about Aiden: an intriguing quality strong enough to make me exchange phone numbers, accept his kiss on the cheek and quite contentedly go home alone.

Back in my bedroom, I kiss my photo of Eoghan good-night and hide it back within its drawer. I tuck the silver frame amidst my underwear: the secret evidence of another life entirely.

Four days later Aiden calls. Like most single women, I'm an ardent call-screener and so, because I don't recognize his number, I don't answer, but he leaves a voicemail asking to take me to dinner on Friday. I'm pleased. And then surprised at the pleasure he's brought me. I text him and accept his invitation. He texts back with the details of a dinner reservation. I panic.

In normal circumstances, this would be a victory: in the normal world where twenty-three-year-olds have only a bum-bag of metaphoric baggage to carry. My baggage, on the other hand, is unfashionably coffinshaped and too big to check into the cloakroom.

With the girls rallying around, I make it until midnight Thursday before I cancel. I am guiltily aware that I will face the wrath of three women in the morning, as my housemates, all single and desperate for boyfriends, believe it a crime to cancel a date when available guys are in such short supply. But the overwhelming voice in my mind is a sensible one: it's too soon to date, isn't it? Sex is different. Like a prostitute who won't kiss her clients, I'm happy to get physical, to connect body to body, but I draw the line at becoming emotionally involved. One-nighters are fine, but dating is very different. To laugh, and joke, and share my thoughts with someone other than Eoghan – that would really be betraying him. Not to mention the fact that, if I begin to date someone regularly at some point, I'll have to tell them. And the 'By the way, I'm a widow' conversation is not one I look forward to.

So I cancel. At midnight on Thursday I text Aiden a transparent excuse that I've come down with the flu. I'm pretty sure he sees straight through my lie, but he has the decency to be polite and says we'll rearrange for another time.

Three days later, it's Sunday evening, and with only soap operas as company, I sit alone, kicking myself for letting nerves get the better of me. I know Aiden plays football nearby on a Sunday and so send him a text to suggest he drop over after the game. Now this boy must be a sucker for punishment because, an hour later, he accepts my invitation.

What I do next is inexcusable. Staring at that text message, my bruised and battered psyche gets the better of me. 'What am I doing? I can't date, I'm a married woman,' I want to scream. Instead I hide: in all senses of the word. I turn off my phone, run to my room, get into bed and pray with paranoid abandonment that there is no way he can guess where I live and ring on the doorbell.

Of course, Aiden never arrives. I stay in that state of unrest until Monday morning, when I switch my phone on to multiple messages that range from the expected: 'Cool, tell me your address and I'll drop over,' to the confused: 'I can't get through on your phone, do you still want to meet?' to the seriously peeved: 'Look, just forget it, babe. I'll see you around.'

I regret it; I kick myself for days after. More than anything, I feel like the cancer has won a point against my self-will: it has made me act rudely, with no consideration for another human's feelings. Eoghan would be ashamed of me. For the first time since his death, I am ashamed of myself.

10 *January 2008*

I settle down on the sofa to read the day's newspaper when the date on the front page catches my eye. With a swift calculation, I realize Eoghan's six-month anniversary passed eight days before. I hadn't known. I feel like I've been punched in the stomach. What sort of person does that make me? What sort of wife? I retrace the week and note with irony that it fell on the Saturday before. A Saturday night I'd spent on the lash, as is traditional for our household. A Saturday night I'd spent with my tongue in a stranger's mouth, as is traditional for me.

Since Eoghan's death, I have prided myself on not conforming to the stereotype of a widow: I never cry on strangers' shoulders and work hard not to be bitter. Most importantly, as a rule, I never play the 'what if?' game – the rules aren't fair, and you're never going to win. Instead, I bolster myself with the belief that everything happens for a reason and the worn and torn cliché of 'what doesn't kill you makes you stronger'. That's what I believe Eoghan's advice to me would be.

Eoghan was a man with a salacious love for life and an energy that even chemo couldn't dampen. In April 2007, the week after we found out the cancer had spread to his brain, he took me away to Kilkenny to surf in the Irish Sea. I was trussed up in a full-body wetsuit as the water was just four degrees, but Eoghan surfed bare-chested in board shorts. And I've never seen a man look so alive.

He still has hair at this point, although it clings on by its last follicles, and he has shaved his facial hair into his favourite style, 'Le Floffe'. Yes, 'Le Floffe' and no, your French isn't rusty. The reason you don't recognize the noun is because it most certainly doesn't exist. But Eoghan was never the type to be restrained by something as prescriptive as the dictionary. No, if there was no adequate word to describe what he desired, he simply made one up for it. 'Le Floffe' was coined in Australia, where, for a little variety, he shaped his facial hair into a new and more imaginative style every few weeks. The 'Le Floffe' was the absolute worst and involved him shaving his upper lip bare then carving two vertical stripes of hair down the side of his mouth and a perfect square on the nub of his chin.

'You look quite ridiculous,' I tell him.

'Where's your sense of humour, Ame?' he replies, grabbing me and nuzzling his 'tache against my cheek.

'Eogh, get off, that's awful. Please shave it off.'

So, of course, he kept it for months, just to annoy me. He even sported 'Le Floffe' the first time he met my parents. That was the thing about Eoghan, he didn't give a damn: what you saw was what you got and you couldn't help but love him for it. His passion for every waking moment is my justification for moving on with my own life: my incentive to live, laugh and not become bitter.

But now, eight days after his missed anniversary, my resolve wavers, and for the first time since moving to London, I crash and burn. I take up residence in the corner of my bedroom, crouched in a foetal ball on the floor. I question every decision I made during his treatment: should I have got a second opinion sooner, should I have insisted they operate when they said it was futile, should I have let him smoke marijuana? Most of all, when the doctors told me Eoghan had two months to live and said I could keep the knowledge from him, should I have told him he was dying? In this moment of doubt, I tear myself apart, wondering if I should have carried the burden for the both of us and spared him.

My housemate Rachel, a forthright Scottish girl, was

always destined to be my closest friend in the house. Don't get me wrong, I love all three girls, but it's Rachel who's my confidante. Within weeks of moving in with her, I counted her as my best friend.

It's Rachel who finds me, surrounded by the evidence of my wallowing: a box of memorabilia that, in normal circumstances, I keep locked, bound and hidden. Out of the box spill his photos, sunglasses and hair gel: a mobile that has his voice stored on the answer phone, a T-shirt worn the day before he died, wrapped in cotton to preserve its odour. These are items so precious I'd enter a burning building to rescue them, but items so painful that it tears my heart in two to look at them.

Rachel stands at my bedroom door and surveys the scene: takes in the crumpled tissues, my blood-red eyes and shaking hands. She crosses the room and bends to my eye level, like a mother stooping to soothe her child.

'This isn't good,' she says simply, and closes the lid of the box.

As soon as the lid slams shut, I feel like I can breathe again. I know this history, this other portion of my life exists, but I don't need to dwell. What's more, as I have just proved, if I do dwell, I will sink. And I've worked too hard to get here to let myself go back there.

'Come on, Ams, let's get you cleaned up,' says Rachel in the bathroom, handing me a scroll of toilet roll. 'You'll be all right, you know. I knew you were a strong one from the day I met you.'

I cup my hands under the cold tap and throw the water over my cheeks. She's right. I know she is. Some people would call it denial, but as I follow Rachel downstairs towards a living room churning with music and laughter, I know that today, in a backwards way, I've taken a step towards recovery.

Two weeks after the great Aiden debacle, I get a text from him out of the blue: 'So, have you decided to stop speaking to me? Can you at least tell me what I did wrong?' it reads.

As I dissect the situation with the girls that evening, we surmise that the old adage must actually be true: treat them mean and they really will stay keen. I wish I'd realized this years ago, when I was actually in the dating market instead of in this widow's limbo. That knowledge could have been useful.

After much deliberation, I text back apologizing. I also invite him to my housemate, Victoria's, thirty-fourth birthday party, which is taking place that weekend at a pub conveniently ten minutes' walk from our house. I figure this is a safe option. I'm back in my comfort zone, with a drunken meeting in a busy social setting. I will have the girls as wing-women, and he is bringing a friend, so at least I can be sure there will be no awkward silences.

That same week, I start a three-month internship at a newly launched fashion magazine, which is unpaid but at least keeps me busy. I need to get out of the house more, I think. And at least I have my widow's pension to pay my rent: a weekly charitable gift of £180 from the good people in the Irish welfare system.

On Thursday, I blow most of this on a little black dress, rationalizing that I should make an effort for the birthday girl but – who am I kidding? – of course it's for Aiden. Alarmingly, I've found myself thinking about him: doodling his name in my notebook at work, checking his Facebook page for updates, and obsessing over girls who've left greetings on his message board. The time I set aside to think, daily, of my husband, is now split 60:40 with Aiden.

On Friday, decked out in our finest, the girls and I head to the pub at the dangerously early hour of 5.30 to meet partygoers coming straight from their offices. All four of us are single, which is both a blessing and a curse. If one of us had a steady boyfriend, there might be some jealousy but, thankfully, all our love lives are as turbulent as each other's. None of us is an angel, but there are different degrees of promiscuity between us, and a sliding scale of morals that leaves me firmly at the bottom. I won't link names to escapades, as I don't think the girls would thank me, but between the four of us we've had our fair share of flings. No matter what happens, we don't judge each other, and I never feel I have to watch my words with them.

Which is why, on the night of Vicky's birthday, I admit to them that I'm shitting myself. This can hardly be classified as a 'date' but it's still more formal an arrangement than I've been used to, and I'm taken off guard by how nervous I feel.

Aiden isn't arriving until eleven – he's going to a friend's gig beforehand – which leaves me with a gaping window of worry-time. With help from the girls and five glasses of free champagne – Victoria works for a firm of barristers, and the belligerent fools think that flashing the cash will get them a shag – I fill this window by drinking, heavily.

Aiden arrives at eleven o'clock on the dot. I spot him first, waiting in line outside the window with a beanie hat pulled low over his eyes and a tentative smile. My stomach jolts and I realize I like him. Five people queue in front of him, and as they pay their entry fee, one by one, I want to tell the bouncer to stall him. I need more time. I'm not ready for a date tonight, or for the actual relationship that may come afterwards. But it's too late now, he's in. As he crosses the room and kisses me on the forehead, I can't run away from the fact that this is the first man since Eoghan I would actually like to see regularly. And this thought floors me.

The next morning, I wake with the dawn chorus, a fur-lined tongue and my platform shoes still on. I fling an arm across the mattress and realize I am alone in bed: suspiciously alone. Then my eyes adjust to the light and my memories jigsaw into place. Fuck! I pull the duvet back over my head, but soon the stench of stale booze drives me from my pit and, pulling a jumper over my now very crumpled little black dress, I trudge down the stairs to the kitchen.

The first person I see is Victoria, swaying unsteadily at the foot of the stairs, her oaky brown hair tousled like a scarecrow's. There's a mop in one hand and a red stain at her feet. I spot Lucy, lying on the kitchen floor behind her, sprawled on her stomach across the kitchen tiles, still wearing the clothes from last night and seemingly asleep; a half-eaten loaf of garlic bread is crumbled on a plate next to her feet. This sight is soothing – a familiar after-party scene. It always comforts me that I'm not the only one unhinged.

'Who spilt bloody red wine?' I ask Victoria.

'Oh my God, Amy, we had to call an ambulance.' Her speech is still slurred from last night's indulgence.

'Someone fell down the stairs on to her head.'

Her voice breaks, but instead of the tears I'd expect, she laughs. I conclude from this that nobody died, so decide to make a cup of tea before asking for details. With a hangover this bad, you have to prioritize, and these dramatic occurrences are common in our house: it's one of the reasons I love it so much. My dead husband is just part of a rich tapestry of oddities.

As the kettle boils, Vicky realizes her cleaning attempt is fruitless and joins me at the kitchen table.

'What happened to you?' she asks. 'You disappeared.'

I sink my head on to the tabletop. 'I ran away,' I groan.

Victoria stares at me steadily but is wise enough not to interrogate me further. She knows I will provide more information eventually.

Two cups of tea and seven chocolate biscuits later, I have the strength to voice my confession.

I tell Vicky how I kissed Aiden at the bar. How his arms were wrapped around me. How I heard my heart beating in my ears. How I felt so special next to him, so wanted again; not sexually, in the red-blooded way men usually look at me, but in a new sense. He looked at me like he wanted me; as a friend, and a lover and more. As a girl-friend? That word became obsolete in my vocabulary a long time ago.

I tell Vicky how I freaked: how I told him I was 'Just popping out to the toilet' before I slipped out the door. Except 'slipped' is the wrong verb entirely: 'slipped' suggests my exit was a smooth manoeuvre. In reality, there was no way Aiden could have missed me drunkenly lurch for my coat, crash out the door of the bar and sprint down the road, a pair of vodka-jelly legs on five-inch heels, desperately trying to hail imaginary taxis, even though my house is in easy walking distance.

This time, Aiden doesn't text me to ask why: maybe my erratic actions no longer surprise him. More likely, he's finally reached his limit.

I place myself in purgatory for the rest of the weekend: send him endless text messages and have numerous phone calls rejected. I can't blame Aiden for cutting me off: any person with a smidgen of self-worth would do the same.

On Sunday night, I lie in bed and cry; I cry because I am painfully lonely, because my bed is too big for one. I cry because, for the first time, I have no idea which man I am missing.

On Monday, I receive a letter from Eoghan's mother. I instantly spot the envelope on the doormat: the Irish postage mark sets it apart from the pile of bank statements and bills. I hold the letter with only my fingertips: scared it could suck me through the ink and take me back there.

In the beginning, I used to phone Ireland once a fortnight, but his mother once confessed she finds it too hard to talk to me: that she hears too much of Eoghan in me. This is the most wonderful compliment I could ever receive, but for her it makes talking to me a strain. As two women united in grief, we have an understanding, and I don't want to make this harder than it need be, so now we write and, secretly, that suits me just fine.

Between me and you, I actively avoid contact with anyone vaguely linked to Eoghan and our old life in Ireland.

I won't answer my phone to Irish country-codes and have given my parents' address to his friends instead of that of my new Islington home. I have been invited back to Dublin for various special occasions – a christening, a birthday party, a wedding – but I make my excuses each time. People seem to understand – or else they wait until my back is turned to criticize.

I'm fully aware that I consciously keep Dublin at a distance. I have a deranged fear that one day someone will force me back there, not only geographically, but to that moment in time: the moment I had to say goodbye.

So his mother and I write, and though the news we share is light-hearted, we read between each other's lines. We don't need to say we miss him; we don't need to say life is monochrome without him. The tearstains on the page say it all.

I sign off each letter with: 'Remember I love you always,' and she knows I'm reassuring them both – mother and son – equally.

Chapter Two

For two whole weeks after Vicky's party I vow off men and do some soul-searching. I consider the possibility that my nonchalant attitude towards the opposite sex is in fact a farce and maybe, just maybe, I'm not as untouchable as I like to believe. I consider the fact that maybe one-night stands are not the best thing for me right now. In fact, maybe I should avoid men in general, and 'love myself', as all the women's magazines say. I rip a piece of paper from the notebook I keep next to my bed for such revelations, and scrawl across it in black marker pen: 'No more men.' I then stick it to my mirror. There.

By 7.30 that evening my feminist resolve has already wavered. Every one of my housemates is out on a date and I'm already in my pyjamas. Maybe swearing off men altogether isn't the answer, I think, unzipping my pencil case and grabbing the marker pen once more.

I scribble through 'Men', then squeeze a few more words on to the poster: 'No more sex. Go on dates,' it now says. Much better, I think. Surely Eoghan wouldn't begrudge me a nice slap-up meal, or being taken to the cinema every now and again.

Shame this realization comes a little too late for me and

41

Aiden. I should have just enjoyed our time together, instead of over-analyzing it and getting myself in a state. Why do I take myself so seriously? No wonder I'm sitting here alone in my pjs, whilst all my friends are out being wined and dined. I stew on this for an hour, staring out of the window into a murky wall of rain. In the end I choose sleep as an escape from the boredom and head to bed before the watershed, taking a shot of Night Nurse to ease me into unconsciousness.

The next morning, the sun is splitting the sky when I wake. I take this as a sign: a new dawn, a new day. I run through the phone book on my mobile. There must be one possible date logged on here, I think, scrolling through the A–Z of names. Faced with a contact book filled with family members, work colleagues and Chinese takeaways, I have to admit there is only one option: Aiden. Oh well, what do I have to lose?

I glance out the kitchen window and see an unbroken horizon of spring-like blue sky.

'Oh what a beautiful morning, oh what a beautiful day, the sun has got his hat on, you can't rain on my parade,' I type merrily. Then, as an afterthought, I write in brackets: 'Add other sunny-day songs as appropriate . . .'

Send.

This text could mean anything. This text he could easily, and expectedly, ignore. But a mere three minutes later my phone beeps with a message alert.

His reply says: 'Hey, crazy face, what you up to?'

I give my brain no time to backtrack, writing quickly: 'Just going to hop on a bus in the vague direction of town. What about you?'

'I'm in Soho for Chinese New Year. Give me a call when you're in West London and we'll meet.'

I wonder if this is a practical joke but push my scepticism aside, slap on some make-up and march out the front door into the sunshine. I don't even change, committing the heinous fashion crime of meeting a man in tracksuit pants. But I know if I allow my mind time to mull, I will cancel before I reach the underground. Eoghan, we are going on a date. This is it.

We arrange to meet under the Carnaby Street archway. I arrive first and lean against the wall, attempting a stance that says, 'I'm casual, I'm cool.'

There are two elements I'm not prepared for. One is for him to be thirty minutes late; the other is for him to bring a companion. Not any companion, but a slim, blonde, girl-shaped tag-along.

'Hi, crazy face.' On the surface his greeting is enthusiastic, but he doesn't lean to kiss me. And, by the way, when did I adopt this nickname? It's not exactly complimentary.

'This is Jenna.' He turns to introduce her, but doesn't elaborate, and I decide not to probe. My fantasy date has already gone up in smoke.

At Aiden's suggestion, we head to a coffee shop, where we are joined by his friend Jacob, a sound engineer at a recording studio in Soho. I have definitely read the situation wrong: this isn't a date, it's a group outing, and suddenly I don't care that I'm dressed in lounge wear. I am happy to learn, however, that Jenna is a colleague from work. Aiden talks about her in platonic tones, but she blushes every time he addresses her directly.

Poor girl, I think, she's smitten, and she's not the only

one. I brush my leg against Aiden's under the melamine-topped table, and he glances my way but doesn't reciprocate. Two rounds of cappuccinos later, Jenna has a hair appointment, the boys realize they're late for a football game and I am silently hurling expletives at Eoghan for letting me get it so wrong.

Jenna heads off to the salon, and the three of us who remain detour to Jacob's studio to pick up his training gear. Security at the studio would put MI5 to shame so, whilst Jacob runs upstairs, Aiden and I linger on the pavement outside. The temperature has been dropping steadily throughout the day, and now my bare arms are raised in goose pimples. My teeth start to chatter and I mutter, 'Can I get in your coat, mister?', more for my own amusement than to get a reaction. I'm long past a charm offensive.

This simple sentence must spark something in Aiden's psyche, as he seems to notice me for the first time. A deep masculine laugh escapes from his throat, and he grabs me roughly round the waist, pulling me within the warm lining of his jacket. He nudges my face with his so we're nose to nose and, as he kisses me, I say to Eoghan: this guy will keep us on our toes.

Since Eoghan died, I have visited a spiritual healer at two-month intervals. Yvonne has been a key figure in my family for the past four years, ever since my father was diagnosed with Hodgkin's Lymphoma in 2004 and reiki was recommended by a friend as a complementary therapy to chemo.

For now, I won't go into the absolute nitty-gritty of my father's illness. I'm sick of the C-word; it angers me, I hate it. Yet I say it so often it's like a common noun in my conversations. My knowledge of cancer is so in depth I could discuss it all day, but I still don't want to. When Eoghan was alive I had reason to, but now he's not, I'd rather avoid it, thank you.

In short, my father was diagnosed just after my twentieth birthday, had chemo, went into remission, then three months later had a colossal relapse. The spreading tumours were only discovered when one, which was growing around the base of his spine, cut off the nerves, and he woke up paralysed.

That first time around, I was at Alton Towers on a sunny August day in 2004 when I got the phone call. My dad, a rower, who prided himself on being sporty and healthy, had driven himself to casualty two days before, complaining of shortness of breath. A virus, we'd thought, or a chest infection at most. Cancer, my sister said.

The word 'cancer', shit, it terrified me back then. To me, cancer equalled death, and the beginning of the end. I coped with my father's illness by being hands-on, sitting in on every treatment and coming home from university at every opportunity to be near him. Whereas my older sister preferred to take a back seat through his illness, I was happiest when the summer holidays started and I never had to leave his side. It doesn't mean either of us loves him less, I know. Sometimes now I wish I hadn't seen so much, hadn't stayed quite so close.

It was after eight months of chemotherapy that he went into remission, and as his body recovered from the treatment, he began to look like my daddy again. He regained the weight he'd lost – he'd become so thin during chemo he could no longer wear his wedding ring – his hair began to grow back, and the colour returned to his cheeks. By April I was back living at university full time, confident it was safe to leave him, but I'd still call home every evening to check on him.

On the second Sunday in May, when I called home, nothing at all seemed out of the ordinary. I phoned around 9 p.m., told my father my news, told him I loved him, and we rang off without a second's thought. Soon after this, my mum and he went off to bed.

That night, I slept though an earthquake. It didn't wake me. And, oddly enough, it was never reported on the news. But there must have been one. Because when I woke, to the ringing of my phone the next morning, my world had cracked in two.

'Hello.' I answer the phone.

'Ame?' says my sister. 'It's Louise.'

My sister doesn't call me in the mornings. This is unheard of; we only ever call in the evenings, after seven, or at weekends, as both our social lives are often hectic. So I know before she starts her next sentence. I wait, silently, for what awful news she has to tell me.

That morning, my father had woken up unable to feel his legs. He was rushed to hospital, where a PET scan showed a tumour had grown around the base of his spine. They would be starting immediate radiotherapy, then back into chemotherapy. Already Stage V, it didn't look good.

'I'm coming home,' I tell Louise, 'I'll meet you at the hospital.'

Rolling my suitcase from under my bed, I pack almost

everything I own. I jump in my little Nissan Micra and drive at blinding speed to the hospital, a journey that usually takes two hours taking less than one. Fuck, no fucking parking spaces, so I leave my car in the motorcycle space of the hospital car park, daring the attendant to give me a ticket. Just try me, I think, you won't know what's hit you if you provoke me today.

I know what room my father will be in. I know this hospital like the back of my hand by now, and as I march up the echoing corridor I prepare myself for the worst. I don't want to look shocked, surprised or alarmed, I must stay calm. Fully expecting a man, half dead, as I stand in the shelter of the doorframe, I'm taken aback – he looks exactly the same.

'Hi, Ame,' he says, appearing only slightly tired. God, what self-control he has. He must have been so terrified.

'Hello, Daddy,' I reply with forced cheer and a smile, crossing the room to kiss his cheek. I don't bother to ask how he is feeling, knowing I won't get the truth anyway. My mum, sitting next to his bed, perched on an un-comfortable plastic chair, reaches out and grips my hand: 'You didn't need to come all this way, love,' she says, a little too sharply. I see a flicker of panic in her eyes and wonder why she doesn't want me there.

Two years later, when my parents flew from England to visit Eoghan, I would mimic her words. 'You didn't need to come all this way,' I'd say, wishing they would go away. Wishing they wouldn't interrupt our time together, when time together was just so precious. But I didn't understand that back then.

I also didn't understand how sick my father really was.

I didn't see he was numbed by morphine, without the drugs in agonizing pain, and utterly terrified. I was so naive. This all changed the next day.

The next day is my dad's first round of radiotherapy, and me and my mum both want to go with him. I'd only seen him lying in bed the day before, and had gone home sure the doctors were exaggerating. I'm sure he can walk really, I thought, I'm sure he's just a little stiff.

I'm out of the room, fetching tea from the canteen, when the nurses manoeuvre him into a wheelchair. By the time I get back into the room, he's sat neatly in the chair, legs covered in a bobbled blanket, looking quite himself. I push his wheelchair down the corridor, making jokes, and revving noises, like he'd do when I was little, running me round the garden in his rust-covered wheelbarrow.

We have to wait for twenty minutes in the radiotherapy waiting room before his appointment. Apparently, there's a backlog of patients because one of the machines had broken down for an hour that morning. My mum has to make a call to work, so steps out into the hospital court-yard. I flick through *Hello!* magazine, idly commenting on the stars of the moment, but neither my dad nor I really know what I'm saying. I can see he is fidgeting; uncom-fortable, uneasy.

'Are you OK?' I ask, after a minute or so.

'Fine,' he replies. But I can see he is lying. His hands grip the metal arms of the wheelchair. Oh God, I think, he's in real pain.

I stare down at my own hands, to avoid looking at his: grasped in my lap, my fingernails digging into the taut, whitened skin on my knuckles. But I can't just sit there.

'Daddy,' I say, 'are you in pain? I'll go and call for the doctor.'

'No,' he snaps, and I jump back, stung. 'Look, it's just . . . I need the toilet, OK? But I don't want you to take me. I'll wait for your mum to get back.'

I peer out the window and see she's far away, on the other side of the garden, deep in conversation, head bowed, and tissue crumpled in her hand.

'There's no point waiting, why don't you just go?' I say. God, I was so young. I couldn't see.

There comes a silence. Then, 'Amy, I can't,' he replies. 'I can't go on my own.' And that's the moment, like a concrete block falling on to me. Thud. I suddenly realize.

'I'll take you,' I say, then, seeing he's about to protest, I repeat, firmer this time, 'Daddy, I'm taking you.'

In the toilet I wrap my arms around his waist. 'Ready,' I say, 'one, two, three,' and with all my strength I pull him upright. Holding my father's full weight in my arms, I realize that he can't support himself at all. I am happy to be standing behind him: that he can't see my eyes screwed up, from both the burning in my arm muscles, and the awful realization of what I'm doing.

'OK,' he says shyly, when he's done, and I lower him back into the wheelchair and fumble to help pull up his pyjama bottoms.

I wheel him back out of the toilet, making a fruitless joke about how I'll soon have arms like the Incredible Hulk. My mum is back in the waiting room, looking panicked.

'Where were you?'

'Just in the toilet,' I say, and then, before she can reply: 'Now I'm crying out for a cup of tea, so I'm just going to pop to the canteen.'

I make it midway down the corridor before I can't hold it back any more. I swerve into the nearest empty room and drop into a chair. I don't cry as I would have in the past. It seems infantile. I have to be stronger now.

That was the day I lost my childhood. The day my barrier against the world went up. The day I realized my father, my protective force, couldn't shelter me any more.

Four gruelling years on, and one stem-cell transplant, he's back in remission, and walking again. I say this tentatively, with fingers crossed and a silent prayer, because it's really just a waiting game. We've been told by the doctors it will strike again one day. It's just a matter of seeing how long it takes to catch up.

My mother, well, she went through the wringer and relies on Prozac to cope with the fear it will come back. My father, on the other hand, says cancer was 'the best and worst thing that ever happened' to him. But then my mother always told me it's harder for the carer than the patient – something I never thought I'd understand first hand.

Before his illness my father was an agnostic who would have scoffed at any psychic. But it is amazing what a near-death experience can do to even the most stubborn man. In desperation, he agreed to a course of reiki – the Japanese technique based on the belief that when spiritual energy is channelled through a practitioner, the patient's spirit is healed, which in turn heals the physical body. He found this so beneficial that he started researching alternative medicine further, and found Yvonne who he now visits frequently for crystal healing. He is like a different man; open, perceptive, in touch with his feelings, and with acceptance of the ups and downs of life. His advice to me and Eoghan was invaluable.

My father is a modest man and would never push his beliefs on to anyone: in fact, he rarely voices them. But I know he goes nowhere without blood stones in his pocket – a quartz believed to be an excellent blood cleanser and a powerful healer. I also know he has no fear of death: firmly believing there to be another life to come after this one.

I mention this now because, the day after I reunite with Aiden, my father calls me with news. He's just returned from a spiritual healing session with a message for me. A message from Eoghan channelled psychically.

Since Eoghan's death Yvonne has passed nuggets of news from Eoghan to me: with such precise and personal detail that I have no doubt it has to be him. By now, I am not shocked by the concept, but to anyone who finds it hard to understand, or just plain terrifying, I describe it as little more than a long-distance telephone call: a chance to catch up with a long-lost friend.

On this occasion Eoghan's message is interspersed with laughter. He wants to tell me he finds it very amusing to watch a certain boy chase me romantically. He says I've run rings around him. And that I should see the reason I'm sabotaging the relationship is because I'm really not ready to move on.

My father relays this message, over the phone. He laughs, and at first I laugh along. Then, after putting the phone down, I begin to feel resentful. Illogically resentful, I know, but the strength of the emotion takes me by surprise all the same.

'How dare Eoghan tell me I'm not ready,' I mutter. 'How dare he try to put me off dating again?' I scowl at the air in front of me, giving my husband's spirit the evil eye. Fuck off, Eoghan, and butt out of my business. It's not your place any more. If you wanted a say, you should have fucking stayed.

I reach for my phone and indignantly punch out a text message to Aiden, too angry to bother with niceties: 'Come over,' it reads. He arrives within the hour, no questions asked. He's come straight from football training; his legs are mottled with mud and his clothes are stained with grass and sweat. Right then his manliness is overpowering. I fuck him for the first time that night. It happens quickly – we're both aware this is why he's been invited here, the obvious next step in our haphazard courtship. I don't bother with formalities – the offer of beer or coffee – but lead him straight into my bedroom, shutting the door firmly behind us. Small talk is also not an option. He's instantly on me, pulling my T-shirt over my head, wrestling to unbutton my jeans, his mouth locked on to mine the whole time. When I'm stripped to my underwear he lifts me over his shoulder, like a fireman, and carries me to the bed, tossing me on to my back on the mattress. There's no foreplay – he pulls his trousers to his knees and then he's in me, his weight leant heavily on me. The sex is angry: punctuated with scratches, hair-pulling and vicious expletives. He flips me on my stomach, and my head smacks repeatedly against the bedpost as he takes me hard from behind. There's something satisfying about the sharp thud of my head against the wood.

Twenty minutes later it's all over. I wasn't even close to orgasm, but then that's not unusual any more. That's not what sex is about with me. I don't care about the climax, I only crave physical contact. Pleasure, pain, it's all the same, as long as I'm feeling something.

The next morning, as Aiden sleeps, I stand naked in the kitchen inspecting my war wounds: a love bite on my neck and the imprints of his nails on my back. I have no idea how I'm feeling. So I poke the purple-tinged bruise on my wrist – just to feel something.

I tiptoe back into my bedroom, careful not to wake Aiden. His face is blocked by pillows, but his snores are regular and reassuring. I stand next to the bed and count his inhalations, out of habit more than conscious action. I used to do this in the last months with Eoghan: aware that any breath could be his last, that any moment could be that moment. The moment it comes to an end. It's funny: in the daytime fear never touched me, but at night, as Eoghan slept, I would be paralysed with dread just waiting for the moment.

Today, I stand over my bed, looking down at the large mound of male laid across the right side of the mattress. I squint. I let myself pretend. It could, maybe, it could be him.

I convince myself that, when I pull back the duvet, his hair will be blond and his face familiar; that a wedding ring will be cradled on his finger.

He coughs, rolls over and dislodges the cushions that

disguise him. Aiden's hair is dark mahogany, his face tanned with oriental genes. He couldn't be less like Eoghan, whose blond hair and glassy white skin gave off his Irish parentage the moment you saw him. It is actually a relief to be forced back into reality.

With my bubble burst, I cut my losses and jump back in bed beside Aiden. Because that's the thing with widowdom: there's no room for denial. Once the lid's on the coffin, closure is unavoidable.

4 July 2007

I have a very hazy memory of Eoghan's funeral. I remember the bulk, but the edges are blurry. It makes me wish I'd had the foresight to ask a relative to film the ceremony. I know it sounds weird, but we do it for weddings after all.

I remember telling exactly this to a distant friend of the family, who'd stopped me in the supermarket to offer her condolences. She didn't quite get it, looked at me worryingly, and scuffled into the sanctuary of the fruit and vegetable aisle, probably scared that my head might start spinning.

But a funeral video is not so perverse. It would be a good resource now, looking back. I was in no place to notice those friends who'd turned up: those who'd travelled internationally and those who'd made their excuses. I can't remember the weather, or whose bouquet was biggest. These things are important, as these are the factors that Eoghan would notice.

But my memories are disjointed. I've blocked out those moments I can't bear to relive.

At the church I sit sandwiched between my sister and a brother of Eoghan's, with his mother on my left and my own family flanking me from behind; like a human wall of support that I desperately lean on to keep me vertical.

I wear a white nightie for the requiem mass. An odd choice, and I can hear people whispering, but in homage to Eoghan's unconformity, I refuse to wear black, point blank. My dress is second hand – saved from a bargain bin in an Australian charity shop – but is saturated with happier memories: stained with Bacardi from a festival in Brisbane, with a rip in the seam where I caught it on my surfboard's fin. I wore it the night Eoghan proposed. This dress symbolized our beginning and I felt it only fitting that I wear it for the ending.

The church is quickly full, and mourners queue down the street outside. I've never seen grown men cry like this: thick-set builders, rugged-faced and musclebound, bawling their eyes out like children, unashamed to tell the world their hearts are breaking.

In the Irish tradition, mourners file past the family of the deceased at the Removal, shaking hands and paying their respects. I'm second in line, so obviously part of the immediate family, but yet the mourners waiting in line look through me. Their eyes jump from Eoghan's mother on my left, to his brother on my right, barely acknowledging me, shivering, in between. I feel invisible.

One stranger, stood directly in front of me, facing me, peers down the church pew then stage-whispers to the women next to her in line: 'Where do you think his wife is? Maybe she couldn't face it, poor love.'

I don't care enough to correct them. I don't have the energy. I want to go home.

However, Eoghan's older brother catches the remark and introduces me, loudly enough for the front half of the church to overhear. Not many disguise their astonishment, and I can hardly blame them. I look too young to be a bride, let alone a widow.

Eoghan's coffin is beautifully over the top: purple lined with elaborate carvings down the side. He wears his wedding suit for the big day. Ever the showman, he would be pleased he looked so suave.

My mum stands up to read the eulogy: originally taken from the book *The Smoke Jumper* by Nicolas Evans, she had pulled it from Sheila Hancock's book, *Just the Two of Us*, about John Thaw. She's had it sandwiched in the pages of her diary for months now. I wonder if she'd saved it with this purpose in mind.

I look down as she begins to read. I don't want to see her face or catch her eye. I hate that she has to do this for me.

'If I be the first of us to die
Let grief not blacken long your sky.
Be bold and modest in your grieving.
There is a change but not a leaving.'

My mind wanders as she continues. I don't want to be here, and don't want to listen to some old poet's words that, to me, mean nothing. Instead I stare at my lap, my pale thighs hidden by a jumble of possessions: items I'd desperately grabbed and brought for comfort: a photo of Eoghan, laughing on our wedding day, a Tasmanian devil teddy bear he'd bought, in Australia Zoo, on my twenty-second birthday, and a scrap of comfort blanket I'd owned since I was a toddler. Now, I bury my hands in the folds of downy fabric, and pray to be a baby again, away from the adult world and the heartbreak it brings.

'And just as death is part of life,
The dead live on forever in the living.
And all the gathered riches of our journey,
The moments shared, the mysteries explored,
The steady layering of intimacy stored,
The things that make us laugh or weep or sing,
The joy of sunlit snow, or first unfurling of the spring,
The wordless language of look and touch,
The knowing,
Each giving and each taking,
These are not flowers that fade,
Nor trees that fall and crumble,
Nor are they stone
For even stone cannot the wind and rain withstand,
And mighty mountain peaks in time reduce to sand.
What we were, we are,
What we had, we have,
A conjoined past imperishably present.'

My mum's voice, so controlled until now, breaks on 'have', and she stumbles on the next line. She pauses, just for a second: a second's silence that catches my attention more than the entire poem. Probably no one else in the congregation even notices, but I know her, I'm a part of her, and know something poignant must be coming. So, finally, I start to listen.

'So when you walk the wood where once we walked
    together,
And scan in vain the dappled bank beside you for my
    shadow,
Or pause where we always did upon the hill to gaze
    across the land,
And spotting something, reach by habit for my hand,
And finding none, feel sorrow start to steal upon you,
Be still.
Close your eyes.
Breathe.
Listen for my footfall in your heart.
I am not gone, but merely walk within you.'

On the fourth line, smack bang on 'hand', I hiccup, so loudly the sound is caught by the air and thrown around the church arches, echoing off the stonework. A valve is released inside me and, though I was sure I had no more tears left in me, a torrent of them follow. I'm crying silently, but my shoulders shake, my body shudders, and the eyes of the congregation, in one movement, spring on to me.

A firm hand is placed on my right shoulder from behind and then another on the left-hand side as Eoghan's closest friends, seated in the second row, reach out to hold me – or maybe to hold the closest thing to Eoghan. My sorrow is infectious – it rushes down their arms, and one by one it breaks them. Their loud, masculine howls put my meeker tears to shame. Like a domino effect, the grief sweeps down the church, from front to back, as one pew after another dissolves, and soon the church is wailing as one. Standing at the front, my mother, somehow, finishes the poem, with a remarkable show of dignity and strength. She leaves the lectern and slowly walks back to her seat, where she collapses silently into my father's waiting arms.

I've never really thanked her for what she did that day, or Eoghan's mother, who organized the whole funeral. I was no help at all in the lead-up. For one, I had no idea what needed to be done, and anyway, I was like a zombie, incapable of making any sensible decisions. I had no input, except – I forget – to choose the parting song. Which is why, as the mass ends and Eoghan's coffin is lifted on the shoulders of his four brothers and two closest friends, the first bars of 'Smile' by Nat King Cole drift out of the speaker system, to send him on his way. Eoghan and I had heard it on the radio a week before he died, and had glanced at each other, making a silent agreement.

With leaden footsteps, the coffin carriers walk down the aisle. Eoghan's mother follows first – dry-eyed and stoical. As the dead man's wife, I am traditionally next in line, but as I rise from my seat I catch sight of the coffin, face on, for the first time. My husband is inside that box, I think. And the room starts to spin. My dad holds my arm on one side, my mum steadies me on the other. 'Don't want to see,' I whisper to them. 'Please, Daddy. Don't make me look at it. I can't.'

I shut my eyes and cover my face with my hands, like

a toddler who believes it will make her invisible. If I can't see, maybe it's not real. As I'm led down the aisle, I feel the eyes of the congregation on me and I'm crushed by the weight of their sympathy. I can never escape this, I realize. This is how it's always going to be.

I watch as the coffin is lowered into the plot. I don't want to see the earth tossed over it, so I stand ten feet away, with my cousin on one side of me and my sister on the other, both of them holding identical stances, with their feet shoulder width apart and legs braced as if they're preparing to catch a great weight – I'm not sure whether that's me or my grief.

Eoghan's coffin hits the top of his father's with a clunk. The priest is speaking but I'm not listening. What else is there to say? I think. Why are we dragging this out? That's just a body in a box down there – it's nothing but meat, it may as well be a carcass we've bought from the butcher's as him. I feel nothing, no attachment, to this grave at all, and I know I will never come back here again. I look around the cemetery at the rows of marbled headstones, laid in perfect symmetry to those in front. As if death is that formulaic, and the daughter who lies buried in that grave could equal the father who lies in the next.

To this day I've never seen Eoghan's headstone, and if you took me to that cemetery again I doubt I'd pick his plot from the line-up. I'm sure the words on his gravestone are fitting – polite, informative and loving – but no three-line inscription can justly describe him, just as this mound of earth can never represent him: it's too plain, too average and not colourful enough, no matter how many posies and wreaths you festoon across the earth.

I won't visit him there: he can come to me instead.

It appears to be over. Coffin laid, people are moving away from the grave. Obediently, I follow them, in single file between the headstones.

'That's pretty,' I say, pointing to a grave from the thirties, the headstone chipped at the edges and speckled with dirt. My sister and cousin shoot a troubled look behind my back, and their unspoken sympathy grazes my shoulder blade as it passes.

'What?' I ask, swivelling my head to eyeball them both. 'It is. It looks comfy and homely and lived in. Much better than some show-home grave you'd be scared to ruffle the grass on.'

'OK, Ame,' says my sister, brushing my fringe from where it hangs over my eye and adopting a tone reserved for babies and puppies. 'But doesn't Eoghan's look nice as well, with all those lovely wreaths and flowers? He'd be pleased, wouldn't he, that it looks so well?'

I look back from where we came and curl my lip. Eoghan wouldn't like this – this isn't his style. Heaped with puffs of pastel flowers, his grave now resembles a giant meringue, too dainty and pretty to be fitting for death. At the head of the plot, a cross stands at attention, as straight as a dart. The corners of the plot have been shovelled so precisely they look like enveloped corners of a hospital bed – the kind that Eoghan hated and I always had to remake to give his feet room to fidget. It's too neat, too formulaic. Eoghan doesn't like this. He dares me to push the cross just off kilter, to rough it up and dishevel his earthen duvet cover.

A few moments later, without really noticing, I've retraced my steps to Eoghan's grave and stopped in the grassy rivet between him and his neighbour. My family have moved a safe distance away, assuming I need a moment to say goodbye.

I don't feel the gust of wind, but the uppermost wreath on Eoghan's grave falls forward, knocking over its neighbour and causing the corsage at the base to roll off the grave completely. It's not a spectacular tumble, and if I wasn't so close I might not even notice the patch of unkempt earth it's uncovered. Dirt that's broken and yellowed with limestone. I am what I am, it says.

Chapter Three

February 2008

Aiden has now stayed over twice, which makes him a first, as since Eoghan died I have never fucked the same man more than once. After our first night of rough and tumble the sex is more delicate and, for me, a little too considerate. I can handle a hard fuck, but I'm not used to 'making love' – all that tenderness weakens your guard. As I say to Aiden that second night: 'Can you just stop being so fucking nice?'

'What? So, you want me to treat you badly?'

Yes, exactly! Because then it won't hurt so much when you eventually leave me. I don't say this, merely think it.

I am even more uneasy with what follows the sex. I am used to men coming, turning and snoring, with five minutes of conversation in between, but Aiden likes to cuddle, to snuggle, to tuck me in his arms in a way that makes me wary. In all other ways our relationship is casual: when it comes to me he's so laid back he's horizontal. He cancels dates, misses phone calls and is generally slack at keeping commitments. But when I do finally get him alone he is putty in my hands. All this toing and froing is proving confusing.

By explaining this I am really laying the groundwork for my excuses, because this time, for womankind, I have done something inexcusable. In one short conversation, I hit Aiden with a double whammy. I not only confessed 'I was once married' but cherried the cake with the immortal phrase, 'I'm only telling you because I do like you.' In the dating game, this is the equivalent to arsenic. And, sure enough, the confession proves an instant killer.

Let me set the crime scene. It's Friday morning and, if either of our bosses asks, we're 'working from home', though he's proving a delightful distraction and I've written two words of my deadlining assignment. After a lazy morning of love-making we sit on the floor of my living room, legs entwined, his shoulder touching mine. We sip hot soup out of matching mugs: a picture of contentment.

I haven't shared a space like this for so long. Don't get me wrong, I have shared many beds, but only for the briefest time – long enough to get the deed done – and the sour smell of sweat and spunk tends to sully any thoughts of romance. With Aiden the scene is pure and clean. It's comforting, intoxicating, and he's the first man I've been with since Eoghan who doesn't rush out the front door at first light the next morning.

'Do you want to know a secret?' I ask him.

'Yes please,' he grins, thinking this is a game.

So I tell.

At first, Aiden covers his shock, staring into his tea cup as I pour out my story. Then, when it's obvious I'm done and waiting for a response, he says he is glad I chose to

64

tell him and that he admires my resilience. It's a line, prob-ably poached from a soap opera or something. We both know it's inauthentic. He wants out, and who can blame him? His hopes of a fun-time girlfriend have gone up in smoke, and even though I can't ladle blame I want to scream, 'I'm still the same.'

He has to leave shortly after: an emergency at work or a saucepan left on the hob, I can't remember. Predictably, he emails me later that evening: one polite paragraph that says he'll be out of contact for the next three weeks, on an unexpected business trip. I calculate he will be away for my twenty-fourth birthday, though we'd made plans to go out for dinner. I write back, civilly, pointing this out, but get no response. I am desperate for reassurance, and have the urge to bleat and question, 'When will I see you again?' But I bite my runaway tongue. I think I've said more then enough already.

And what did I learn? That next time I'll wait longer. Until our silver wedding anniversary, perhaps, because in the dating game sharing is *not* caring.

11 *May 2007*

As you may have noticed, I have always believed that honesty is the best policy: even if the truth makes others feel uneasy. It was my choice to tell Eoghan he was terminal: that he had two months left at the most. It is a choice that, looking back, I wouldn't change.

On the second Friday in May, Eoghan and I sit in chemo discussing our wedding. This involves the usual animated debates: top hats versus bowler, DJ versus swing band, champagne versus cider – the latter was my fiancé's suggestion. We had set a date for the following summer, and planning the event was a welcome distraction: a way to fill the eight hours it takes for his chemotherapy drugs to be administered. The day ward in the Mater Hospital in Dublin has been designed with comfort in mind: homely and as inviting as an oncology ward can be, with leather recliners and a widescreen television mounted on the wall above the nurses' station. Stools are provided for visitors, but I always sit on the arm of Eoghan's chair, in as close proximity as his intravenous drips allow.

You'll find us here, every twenty-one days, and sometimes in between for blood tests. These trips become the norm very quickly and, you may be surprised to hear, these really were happy times. We often joked that, if you watched us, a young couple stealing kisses when the nurses weren't looking, you would think we were worriless. You might even envy us. Those long days of chemotherapy, some lasting ten hours, are never wasted. We talk non-stop, often to the irritation of the other patients, who want peace. We loudly, excitedly, plan our future: choose Canada as our next holiday destination, decide two daughters would be perfect, and that one day we'll open a surf school in Donegal. We have all the time in the world – we thought.

Until the eleventh of May, when everything changed.

Today, the consultant stops me on my route back from the hospital cafeteria: a canteen thrown back from the eighties, with melamine chairs in a repulsive shade of tangerine and textured wallpaper that peels off the wall at its corners. I used to hate this place, but in the next few weeks, as Eoghan deteriorates and I give up all else to spend twenty-four hours a day at the hospital, this canteen becomes my sanctuary. The place I go to call my parents when I need a break from the hospital ward, and every-thing it represents. Where I sit for an hour, stirring eight sugars into a cup of tea I'll never drink, or cutting the crusts from a sandwich, trying to make the edges line up with perfect symmetry. Here there are distractions I welcome.

Today, Eoghan has sent me down for a newspaper and an ice cream. Chemo makes him crave '99' cones – the kind you buy from old-fashioned ice-cream vans, with a chocolate flake and strawberry sauce that drips through your fingers. Chemo leaves a metallic taste in the mouth, and ice cream's better then a mint, so he says. When I reach the cafeteria there's a handwritten sign propped on the ice-cream machine reading 'Out of Order'. I hover over the freezer cabinet, weighing up the pros and cons of a Magnum versus a Cornetto. What a wonderfully friv-olous decision. I wish I could go back there now, tap myself on the shoulder and say: relish this, this moment, when choosing between two types of ice cream was your most taxing decision. Less than five minutes later, as I walk back to the ward – with a mint-chocolate Cornetto, in case you cared to know – Eoghan's consultant intercepts me, calling my name as I walk past his private office.

'Amy, I've been meaning to speak to you. Could I have a private word – away from Eoghan?'

'OK,' I reply, stopping my brain mid-thought before I panic: not wanting to second-guess what this means. But there's no avoiding the obvious as he leads me down the corridor, to a room I know only too well. Every hospital has a room like this one: an area tucked away from the rest of the ward, with a soundproof door and a box of tissues ready and waiting on the table. Like a calf that recognizes the gates of the slaughterhouse, I can feel my heart beat faster as I walk towards the door, knowing that, once I cross the threshold, once he settles me compassionately in the cushioned armchair, this doctor will shoot me right between the eyeballs with a pellet of devastating news. I won't stand a chance of survival. But still, obediently, I follow him in, my eyes fixed on a ruby-red stain on the tail of his white coat, the silhouette reminiscent of a pitchfork. He gestures to the chair and I sit.

It was in this room that we'd been told the first round of chemo had failed, then later that two tumours had spread to Eoghan's brain. Normally, there are two of us here, to scaffold each other, one of us always finding the right words when the other has run out of speech. But today it's just me, and my mind flickers over the thought: It must be worse this time, but how?

I soon find out. The doctor folds his hands across his lap. He then tells me that Eoghan has about two months to live. It is an approximation, of course, but his estimate proves to be terrifyingly accurate, almost to the day.

'The human brain can only take one series of radiotherapy in a lifetime,' the consultant explains. 'We've tried that, but the tumours have been unresponsive, and it appears from Eoghan's side effects – his loss of balance, the blurring in his right eye, that the tumours are expanding and the pressure on his brain is increasing.'

I already know they can't operate on these tumours because there's more than one cancerous spot, and it would be too dangerous. I also know it is rare for a brain tumour to respond to chemotherapy, as the brain's cell membrane is too thick for it to cross from the blood supply. In other words, we've exhausted all options.

Reading my mind, or at least the desolate look in my eyes, the consultant says: 'I'm sorry, Amy. None of us wanted it to come to this.'

'Is there any chance?' I ask.

'No, Amy, not now.'

I try to inhale, but my chest can't suck in any air. My skin bristles and tightens, like it's lost all elasticity and strains over my bones, suffocates my organs. My fingers claw at my chest, desperate to rip my skin apart, to find a release.

The doctor is still talking, and I wonder what on earth there can be to say: 'I'm telling you this because I can't let you plan a wedding for next year.' He pauses, and the silence is so loud it pierces my eardrums: 'Eoghan won't be here,' he finishes.

A wave washes over me, but it's not unpleasant – like jumping headfirst in the icy surf on a boiling-hot day, it revives me. Relief. That's what I feel now. I didn't realize before that I'd been waiting for this news: always on edge, every time a consultant walked by. Waiting and waiting for that conversation, which would signal the end of the fight. The final punch had been thrown, and I was out for the count. It was time to step out of the boxing ring.

I thanked the doctor, who was hovering an inch off his chair, not sure whether to leave me or to stay and comfort me. But there was no comfort to be given. I hadn't even shed one tear.

'I better get back to Eogh,' I say, and as I say his name, I hear his voice, his laugh, his joy as he tells the nurses: 'Do you know I'm getting married next year?'

I turn to the doctor. 'Please let me tell him,' I plead. 'I don't want him to hear it from anyone else but me.'

'You don't need to tell him at all.' The doctor's response surprises me. 'It's your decision, Amy, but it may be easier not to.'

I look down at my lap, where a mint Cornetto lies, melting gently over my bare thighs.

After leaving the room I walk the length of the hospital corridor, ducking under the window of the out-patients ward so Eoghan won't see me go by, and pause at the floor-length windows that overlook the hospital car park. Outside, there's glorious sunshine: it's the first day of good weather we've had this summer, and I think, How ironic that it should coincide with this. Though I'm wearing a thick, knitted cardigan, my shoulders shiver and my fingers are ice cold. My whole body is numb; it isn't my own. I press my cheek to the window, where the dirt on the glass is monogrammed by the sunlight. I beg the sun to strengthen me, to warm the blood that runs, ice cold, like mercury through me, but the news I've just heard has cast a dense shadow, and blocks the light completely.

The next three hours are without doubt the hardest of my life. Eoghan having an afternoon of treatment ahead, I can do nothing but return to the ward and wait. I have already decided to tell him. It was less a decision and more the only option. I know I can't carry this weight on my own and go on pretending that nothing has changed. But a bustling oncology ward is not the place to tell him this. I won't tell him in the hospital: it's too morbid and too final, with the hospital morgue in the basement beneath us. I have to pick the right moment – away from this place, when it's just the two of us.

So for the next three hours, as I listen to Eoghan plan a wedding for a summer he won't live to see, I sit next to him and fix a smile on my lips. In my head a clock ticks. By the time the last bag of chemo is empty my worry has manifested into a physical agony: my stomach cramps, my head throbs and my throat hurts when I swallow. Eoghan is oblivious to this. The irony is he is feeling well today, better than he's been in weeks. The nausea has faded, the lethargy has passed and if I didn't know better I would say he is over the worst. It makes the news even harder to believe.

On the drive home he sings rapturously along to the radio, tapping a beat on the dashboard with his fingertips.

He cranks down the passenger window and sticks his head out like a crazed puppy, the wind catching the folds of his bandana and nearly ripping it from his head. He steadies it with one hand, laughing.

'What an amazing day, Amox,' he says, drawing his head back into the car, his eyes watering from the drag: 'Can you remember a more beautiful day than this?'

'No, Eoghs, I can't.' Well, what else can I say?

'Drive along the beach way, Ames. We shouldn't waste a day like this driving through the city.'

So I take the next left, joining the road that leads along

the Dublin coastline. I hope the sight of the sea will calm my nerves, and it does, slightly.

Then I remember that two of Eoghan's friends are back at our house, plumbing a new washing machine into our kitchen. They're doing us a favour, and it was me that asked them over but, today of all days, that's all I need. I know they'll stay all afternoon; drinking tea and watching TV, too unobservant to pick up on any hints that they should leave. This means I have a half-hour window to tell him now, or else it'll be this evening, and I don't want to tell him after the sun's gone down. I need the daylight to make the news less intimidating.

Eoghan, you're dying. I run the sentence through my mind. My fiancé is dying. My hands start to shake and I wrap my fingers around the steering wheel to steady them, praying Eoghan won't notice.

I needn't have worried – he's staring out the window, transfixed by a kite surfer leap-frogging the waves in Dun Laoghaire bay. A ferry sails its way lazily across the horizon, starting the journey from Dublin Port to Holyhead in Wales. I'll be doing that soon, I think. After he's gone, I'll take that boat back home to England. Dread settles in my stomach at the thought of starting my life again.

Eoghan turns to face me, looking animated. Though I still feel stone-cold, his face is flushed from the heat of the car and his eyelashes are clumped together with sweat. As the people we drive past are dressed in shorts and T-shirts, I conclude it's with me that something's amiss, not him.

Where on earth is the right place to tell him? I think.

'I think we should go and see Barry,' he says.

In spite of myself, I can't help but smile, because this is so typically Eoghan. Without knowing I need him, he has stepped up to support me. Without hearing my question, he has offered up the perfect answer.

I nod, saving my words for what has to, very soon, be said. As we drive into Dalkey I take a sharp left turn, down a narrow road that only locals really know. It brings us to Bullock harbour and to a secret spot Eoghan and I like to think of as our own. Barry is there – not a person, but one of a family of sea lions who can often be spotted somersaulting in the shallow water of the harbour. Eoghan and I have passed many happy hours sitting here, watching this sea lion, totally absorbed. I wonder why I didn't think of here before.

We settle on a wooden bench on the edge of the harbour wall. Eoghan drapes an arm across my shoulder and idly pulls the sticking plaster from his elbow, where his IV drip was inserted. Beneath the plaster there's no mark, not even a scratch, and I wonder if any of this is real. We sit in silence, until I have to break it. The words I've held in my stomach since lunchtime rise up my oesophagus, and I taste them as acidic bile on my tongue. If I don't tell Eoghan now, if I don't spit this out quickly, I'm in danger of vomiting the prognosis over him.

'Eoghan. Can you look at me a moment? I need to tell you something. It's important.'

I wonder at what moment he knows he is dying: if he reads it in my eyes the instant he faces me or if it falls into place with each sentence:

'Doctor O'Gorman asked if he could talk to me today while you were in chemo.'

'He told me they won't ever be able to do another round of radiotherapy on your brain, even though it seems the first lot didn't work.'

'They had to tell me the worst-case scenario, Eogh.'

'They heard us planning the wedding. They wanted to warn us. To make us prepared.'

That must have done it, as here Eoghan cuts me off.

'How long do I have, Amy?' he asks flatly. 'One year? Five years?'

'Two. Months,' I say.

There's no point in sugar-coating the words. That's it, I think, it's won. I wasn't strong enough to save him.

'They told me you're dying,' I say. As the words leave my lips my head drops into my hands and I vomit through my knees.

Eoghan drags me upright, his fingernails digging into my shoulders as he holds me at arm's length.

'Look at me, Amy.' His voice is stern. When I raise my bloodshot eyes to his, his irises seem bluer than I remember.

'I am not going to leave you,' he tells me, pausing between each word to let it penetrate.

'I swear I am not going to leave you, Amy. I didn't wait this long to find you to lose you now. I promise you, I'm not going anywhere.'

His stoic grip on me tightens.

'You just have to trust me,' he says, and leans forward to kiss my forehead.

It is hard to explain how this happened. Even replaying the conversation here, I'm second-guessing myself. Could it have been this nondescript? I've wondered if my mind has erased his terror. But after picking apart my memory bank, I realized this is exactly as it was. His courage never wavered and, because I trusted him implicitly, at that moment I had a renewed hope. I believed that he could beat it. I believed we'd prove the doctors wrong.

'I love you,' I tell him, because this feels like the right thing to say and because I do.

'I love you too, Amy.' His voice shivers ever so slightly when he says my name. 'And I mean it, we'll find a way to beat it. We will. They don't know me – they're only estimating what will happen from statistics, but when have we ever conformed to the norm? They don't know what they're up against. I'll beat it, Amox. I'll beat it for us. I swear to you, I will.'

We sit on that bench for what feels like hours, but is probably less than one. I would love to tell you now what was running through Eoghan's mind, but I was too scared to probe him, in case he admitted to feeling just as scared. Instead, I sit, look out to sea, and my hope rises and falls with the waves. I want to believe him, but can see the odds are stacked against him, and I've got too much knowledge of cancer to take his survival as a given.

I wonder how the sun could go on shining, and how come the people walking by are still talking and laughing. Don't they know? Haven't they heard what we've been told? It was my first lesson that life always goes on, regardless of whether your little corner of it has collapsed.

That evening, we tell Eoghan's family. There's little point putting it off, especially when time isn't on our side. We call and ask his mother and three brothers to drop round. As soon as they are in the door, and sitting, bunched shoulder to shoulder in a circle of chairs in our tiny living room, I tell them. I can't wait, and this isn't the time for small talk. I have to say the words, to spit the poisonous sentence out: it sits on the tip of my tongue, burning and blistering my mouth.

'The doctors told me today, if the chemo continues as it is, the worst-case scenario is Eoghan has two months left.'

One brother starts firing off questions – the what, the when, the why, why, whys? One brother sits in silence, the other starts crying into his hands. Eoghan's mother, elegant at seventy-five with her silvery hair tied up into a chignon, looks at me with begging questions in her eyes: is it true, is there not anything we can do? I wish I could answer her hopefully, but I have no answers left.

Eoghan sits on a stool in the corner of the room, out of the glaring spotlights, a safe distance away from the inquisition. He'd asked me to tell them, saying I'd find the best way and right words, but now I curse him for over-estimating my ability. I can't do this. I don't know how to sugar-coat such news.

'That's the worst-case scenario though,' I start, wondering how it's been left to me to paint a bright side. 'But new medical breakthroughs are happening every day. Look at my dad; he was cured by a stem-cell transplant that wasn't even discovered when he was first diagnosed three years before. And with alternative therapies anything is possible. Plus –' I'm babbling now, but I don't know how to draw the sentence to a close – 'Plus . . .' Now, I run out of words. I want to say, I'm only joking: he's cured, he's actually in remission. Ha ha, I had you fooled. But as I can't, I stop talking, knowing nothing I can say will be enough.

Later, I stand at the window, watching them leave. They weave down the pebbled pathway of our garden, in single file, like a funeral procession, each with their hands clasped in prayer, and heads bowed. When they reach the row of parked cars in the driveway his mother's knees buckle and a brother catches her as she drops to the ground.

Ten days later, during Eoghan's next dose of chemo, I return from the bathroom to hear the pensioner seated next to him lean to ask him: 'Have you ever considered euthanasia?'

I freeze in the doorway. I'm petrified of who raised this topic in the first place and also of hearing the response on the tip of my fiancé's tongue. A clock ticks behind me, and I think, Come on then, answer him.

'What?' bellows Eoghan, but to my astonishment he's laughing. 'Have you seen who I'm marrying? Who'd choose to die when they've got so much to live for?'

That's Eoghan in a nutshell. That's why I thought we stood a chance.

Chapter Four

March 2008

An article about me was published in the *Mail on Sunday*'s *You* magazine today, with the headline: 'A wife for a month, a widow at 23.' Unfortunately, I wrote the piece five weeks after Eoghan died, but it wasn't published until eight months on, so it really isn't a true reflection of how I now feel. Indeed, it's moping and morbid and totally blinkered: filled with how much I love him, and how I'll never meet a man like him again. I think: If only I had the chance, I'd write a very different story.

But, of course, everyone loves a tear-jerking tale, and my phone has rung red since the magazine hit the shelves. My family are proud as punch and can't understand why I feel so uneasy. If you want me to be honest, I am sick to the stomach. I cringe when I read the sentence: 'I can't go back to being a normal girl about town after this, and that gives me the lonely sense that I don't really belong.' God, what a hypocrite I am, when just last night I was out with the girls, laughing and dancing and kissing a stranger on the dance floor. What a fake, what a fucking fraud I am.

'I do go out with friends every now and then, and I'd be stupid to say that I never want to meet anyone else, but that's too far away to think about seriously. Now, I find myself just staring at other couples, happy, in love, absorbed in one another, just as we were.'

Oh God, I sound pathetic. So naively love-struck: like a sixteen-year-old with her first real crush. When was I ever that in love? I don't even remember it now. I only remember the bad times. It's so much easier to hate him than love him.

'I wake up for him, walk for him, laugh for him; it's thoughts of Eoghan that pull me through the days.'

I hope Tyler doesn't read this and run.

Tyler is a stage name for the new man I am seeing. It's been three weeks since I verbally bomb-shelled Aiden, and though he has emailed me a few times since then there's been no further suggestion of us meeting. His emails are upbeat and always polite but undeniably platonic, with 'babe' swapped for 'mate' as a term of endearment. I take this as a sign that we've crossed the line between lovers and friends.

But, as Rachel keeps telling me, her thick Scottish lilt making it sound even brasher: 'The best way to get over one man is to get under another.' And so I do. I meet Tyler at the Living Room cocktail bar in Islington on the first of March – it's my twenty-fourth birthday and my first birthday without Eoghan. My friends have been making a fuss of me, worrying that on my first birthday minus Eoghan I might go a bit wobbly. To be honest, I had exactly the same fears but, determined to not get down for the sake of it, I have managed to keep him pushed to the back of my mind, and I'm doing just fine.

Champagne cocktails help, of course. In fact, I sink enough cocktails that, the next day, although I can remember making a new 'friend', I have no recollection of his name. I *do* remember: (a) what he does for a living, and (b) his favourite sexual position. The first of these points earns him his nickname. Tyler strangely suits him anyway, so from that evening, it was how we knew him.

Tyler is an Italian-bred cockney with an attractive arrogance and a cheeky smile that makes you forgive him anything. We meet as he crosses the cocktail-bar dance floor. I pull a lollipop – the type the toilet attendants swap for loose change – out of his mouth and put it into my own, before planting it back between his shell-shocked lips.

We bypass small talk; there is barely time for introductions. Our conversation swims on double entendres and, before I know it, we're kissing. I would love to give you more of a run-down. It's not that I'm secretive of my seduction technique; it's more I can't remember how we got to that point.

'Can I come home with you?' he asks, before I get time to proposition him.

'OK,' I reply, and without conferring we both make for the door, not wanting to waste another moment in the overcrowded bar.

As the girls are still out celebrating my birthday, the house is empty when Tyler and I get back. They were too drunk by this stage to mind my early exit and had promised to raise a glass or two more to the birthday girl after I'd gone. They won't be back for hours.

I unlock the door and lead the way down to the kitchen, in the basement. The bottom floor of the house is my favourite: an open-plan living room and large modern kitchen, with clean marble surfaces and minimal clutter, mainly because none of us actually cooks in it.

'Do you want a drink?' I ask, making for the kettle.

'No.' I jump. His mouth is next to my ear. I spin round to face him. He stands directly in front of me, pinning me against the kitchen counter. He kisses me, and I cup the sides of his face in my hands. He lifts me until I'm sitting on the kitchen counter, my legs circling his waist. At first his kisses are soft, affectionate. I don't know if I like this – it's a little too intimate. I drive my tongue deep into his mouth and move my hands into his hair, winding strands through my fingers and tugging lightly. He growls. And suddenly the pace shifts. Tugging at the straps of my top, he rips the material in two. I'm still perched on the kitchen worktop and he tips me backwards, so my legs are straddling his shoulders, my skirt bunched around my waist. Then he's fucking me. Jesus, he fucks me hard. It's a relief to be dominated, to be free of choice and responsibility. A part of me knows that even if I asked him to stop he wouldn't. He's like a hurricane.

He pauses long enough to lift me off the worktop and manoeuvre me on to my back on the kitchen floor. With his weight landing on top of me, my spine hits the lino, hard. I moan with pain, but he doesn't break his rhythm and, minutes later, he comes, with great shuddering convulsions.

I lay on my back, a smile on my face and a sense of achievement. See, I think, I told them I don't need to be handled with kid gloves. I'm not as fragile as everyone thinks I am. I can handle this; I can hold my own in the big bad world.

Tyler, who's standing by now and back in his trousers, holds out a hand and pulls me to my feet.

'Are you staying?' I ask.

'No,' he replies. 'I better get going.'

I walk him to the door, kiss him goodbye and go back to the kitchen to disinfect the surfaces. Then I make a cup of tea and crawl into bed, kissing the air – and my husband – goodnight.

The next morning I don't feel any guilt about last night's conquest. I've started to think of these one-night stands as my form of therapy. Each man is a small tab of Prozac that peps me up and keeps me functioning. Some widows turn to drugs, some turn to alcohol; some have years of expensive counselling at the tax payer's expense. We each do what we must to get by. Instead of wasting time on guilt, I fondly remember the scene in the kitchen and how nice it was to be taken charge of. In that last year with Eoghan, the responsibility of his illness nearly killed me.

13 May 2007

I can't get it right all the time.

I left it too late and, by the time I realized, dehydration had made Eoghan delirious. He had been throwing up for three days straight, and I phoned the district nurse, but she assured me it was normal for the strength of his chemo. She said he could stay at home as long as his temperature remained in the safe zone.

By the fourth day we were both exhausted and, I am ashamed to say, I wished they would just come and take him away. I didn't want to be in charge any more.

The final straw came when he wet the bed. He was totally oblivious, in such a state of disarray he didn't know what he was doing any more. For a moment, I envied him. I was only too aware this was not a good sign. I picked up the phone and finally called an ambulance.

The paramedics arrived promptly and hooked Eoghan straight up to a saline IV. They asked him questions to hold his attention, but he spoke in tongues, his words blurred together into one. When we arrived at the hospital he was admitted to a private room on the oncology ward and, after an examination, his consultant upped his dose of steroids and gave him a blood transfusion.

'His loss of balance and general confusion are significant,' the doctor explained. 'It is most likely that the tumours on his brain are swelling.'

It was midnight by then, and all visitors were asked to leave the ward. I kissed Eoghan goodnight but, though his eyes were open, he didn't seem to recognize me.

I headed home alone, to be greeted with squalor, the stench of sick and an unmade bed stained with urine. I had no strength to clean so slept in a ball on the sofa, a blanket pulled around my shoulders. I didn't want the responsibility of this. I wanted my mum, and yet I wouldn't and couldn't ask for more help. My parents were in London, and though they were my rock, emotionally, they couldn't support me physically. And Eoghan's mother was in her mid-seventies and had already lost one son, who drowned in his twenties. I felt a need to protect her and shield her.

More than that, I had something to prove to his family and friends, who had heard, even before Eoghan was diagnosed, how I'd cared for my dad through his cancer. They'd been told, by my extremely proud husband, how I'd taken my father to chemo, shaved his head, fed him and nursed him, whilst my mum went out to work. They'd heard how my father had, not so long ago, been at death's door, and had fought back into remission. And they prayed, with all their hearts, that I could do the same for Eoghan.

I didn't want to let them down. I wanted to believe I could save him. So I told his friends not to worry, that I could handle it, that it was nothing I hadn't seen before. But, in truth, it overwhelmed me.

When Eoghan and I first met in Australia, I'd agreed to be his girlfriend, then later fiancée, with the promise of a life full of laughter and adventures together. All this had to change following his diagnosis, when I became a carer, a chauffeur, a nurse and a cleaner. Nearer the end, I was more his mother than his partner. I drove him to treatments, planned his diet, sterilized the house and administered his pills: not a simple task in itself, with hourly medicines, supplements and detox drinks, each with specialist instructions.

His appetite was fickle; one day's cravings were the next day's trigger foods and their odour alone would make him vomit. I had to ensure he ate a high-fat diet with as much cream, butter and full-fat milk as he could stomach to counteract the debilitating effect of his treatment. He'd even take his morning pills with a glass of full-fat custard. That was on his good days, when he could stomach something so rich. On his bad days, when the nausea came in consecutive waves, I would hold him upright in bed with a sick bowl between us, taking his temperature at half-hour intervals and trying to guess when an ambulance should be called.

Caring for your father is one thing. But caring for your husband – well, that's quite another thing entirely. I thought it would be easier this time around, if anything, not harder. But I underestimated it wildly. Because, this time around, I wouldn't just lose one person, a father, I'd lose a husband, a lover, a best friend, a soul mate, and with that my hopes for the future, my dreams.

By May, when the cancer spread to his brain, Eoghan was no longer my partner or my equal. He needed me too much, needed me too ardently. And, like an overprotective mother, my absolute love for him meant I couldn't – wouldn't – ask for help from anyone. I couldn't trust anyone to care for him like I did, not even his family.

The Monday after I meet Tyler, my doorbell rings at 6 p.m. I'm just back from the gym and about to jump in the shower, but as all the other girls are still out at work, I throw a towel around myself and amble to the door. I open it to find Tyler, still dressed in his work clothes, spattered with plaster. He grins and looks surprisingly and endearingly shy.

'Hi,' he says, 'I thought I'd drop by after the other night. Just to see how you are.'

I feel myself blushing and wrap my towel more tightly around me, which is a ridiculous reflex action, seeing as this man has already seen me slap-bang naked.

'Umm, come in,' I stutter. 'It's nice to see you.' God, I wish I could remember his name; this is shameful.

I go to walk down the stairs, but as we pass the open door to my bedroom he looks inside.

'So, is this your room?' he asks.

'Yep,' I reply, hastily scanning the room for embarrassing possessions: dirty knickers, misplaced tampons, rogue Harry Potter novels. Thankfully, it all seems presentable.

He steps inside and looks around.

'Nice set-up,' he says, opening my shutters to peer out the window. 'It's a shame we never quite made it this far the other night.'

I laugh, and my nerves instantly fade. 'No, we didn't,' I reply. 'I don't think my kitchen has ever seen that much action. I had to get the disinfectant out afterwards. You're a health and safety risk if ever I saw one.'

He turns to look at me directly: 'You're amazing, Amy.'

He can't mean I'm an amazing person – he doesn't even know me – he means I'm an amazing fuck, which isn't really anything to boast about. But still, that's all it takes to convince me I like him, to convince me to kiss him. One sentence of backhanded flattery, and I'm his again. That's the type of person I am now.

This time we do it doggy-style. As Tyler comes, bareback, inside me, I fall forward with the force and reach for an object to steady myself. The palms of my hands smack against the pine top of my dresser and everything resting on its surface goes flying, across the carpet. Books, make-up and two scented candles smash on to the floor, and the last thing to fall is a cardboard box I had forgotten was even there: a royal-blue box the size of a pack of playing cards filled with love letters written by Eoghan throughout our relationship that I have carefully folded and lovingly saved. The lid falls off the box on its way to the floor and notes float out like confetti: scraps of paper covered in Eoghan's unmistakable scrawl.

I peel myself off Tyler and hastily kick the heap of debris under my bed before he gets the chance to see. As I stand upright, excess semen drips from between my legs and drops on to the note on top, smudging the ink like a teardrop. And I wonder: what on earth have I become?

An hour later I'm alone again and I shuffle under the bed on my stomach to retrieve my fallen possessions. I sit on the carpet, with my back against the bedframe, and choose a letter at random. It reads:

My beautiful Amy. Well, what can I say? I have never come close to the deep sense of happiness and warmth that I feel with you by my side. Because of you I have made my peace with the world and am no longer angry, just looking forward to this fight. I'm ready to take on this battle with cancer. It can take my body and batter it and squash it but it will never ever put out the light that keeps our love burning so brightly. Cancer is just a word to me, not a feeling or an emotion, and it can never take away what I feel for you.

I live to fight the good fight with my beautiful fiancée by my side. I have always and will always dig deeper into myself to do whatever I can to guarantee our right to a future: a future full of happiness, laughter, dancing and echoes of I love you. I promise you that.

He has signed off what will be the last letter he writes me. Yours always, Eoghan.

I had forgotten this letter existed. Eoghan had written it in our last house in Ireland and tucked it inside my shoe one morning before a hospital appointment. From my memory of the glorious weather that day, it must have been mid-June, just weeks before he died.

Back then I took these letters for granted. I never thought they would be all I had left.

I don't cry as I read the note now. I can't cry any more for him. But my hands shake as I refold the letter and put it back in its case.

My phone beeps with news of a text message. The sender is Tyler and his text says: 'You're one fantastic fuck.'

That's it. Nothing more and nothing less. I've become the sole sum of my sexual organs. I wonder where it all went wrong. When did sex become my only talent, the one good thing I have to offer? I'm sure, in my life before cancer, I was more than that.

Wife, widow, 'fantastic fuck'. That's the route I've taken, and with each new noun I lose a little more importance. Deep down, I know it's my fault entirely. How can men compliment anything else about me when I don't give them the chance to know me? I give them nothing to go on, to work with. But I tried, Eoghan, I really did. With Aiden, remember, I tried to share, and he about-turned and ran a mile. Because the true me is just too terrible to cope with, my past too uncomfortable to handle. I can't talk about my past, my family, or what's moulded me. Which leaves me just sex. Safe and uncomplicated.

On 15 March we have organized a house party for Rachel's thirtieth birthday. It's the first party we've had in our Islington home, so we push the boat out, in spectacular style, for the occasion. Rachel is one of those people you can't help but like on meeting. She has the rare ability always to see the best in people – sometimes to her detriment. She's been single for years, and I don't know why she wasn't snapped up long ago, but it never seems to get her down. Unlike the rest of us, who moan and rant about how 'there's no good men left', she simply gets her glad rags on and hits the town: man or no man, she always seems to have a better night than everyone else around. So I know, with no doubt, this party will be a success.

On Rachel's request, the theme is 'Black, Bling and Swing' – as in the dress code and genre of music, before you ask. This is not, as some guests query, a swingers party – although you never know.

We decorate the house from top to bottom, with a red carpet leading up the candle-lined front path and a disco ball hanging from the living-room ceiling. My dress is short and made up of black chiffon tiers like that of a 1930s flapper girl. Rachel looks fabulous, in a full-length, strapless ball gown with a cupid neckline. To contradict all that glamour, we hire a fifteen-foot bouncy castle, which fills the back garden, wall to wall.

I invite both Tyler and Aiden, predicting neither will actually come, but am amazed, and a little disturbed, when they both RSVP their attendance. An hour before the guests start arriving, I decide to stop worrying. What will be will be, and they probably won't even show. Aiden is notoriously unreliable, as I know.

By ten o'clock the party's in full swing and our house is full of drunken revellers. The first surprise of the evening is when Aiden arrives, looking uncomfortable in a tuxedo, which sadly doesn't suit him in the slightest. He heads straight for me, pushes a box of chocolates into my hand and kisses me smack-bang on the mouth. What the hell's going on? He's acting like nothing has happened, like he hasn't ignored me for the past how-many weeks. He scans the basement of our house, checking out the guests, and then loops his arm around my waist. I get the feeling he's marking his territory, which he has no right to do, since he's spent weeks cold-shouldering me. I sidle away, muttering that I need to circulate, and he doesn't follow me, but I see him watching as I weave between men on the dance floor.

The second surprise of the evening comes around midnight when Tyler, who I had long given up on, arrives with his best mate, Ryan, in tow. By this point I have sunk rather more vodkas than planned, and when he spots me I am standing on our teetering coffee table, leading a cancan. Not quite the sleek impression I had hoped to project but, oh well, he already knows I'm a fun-time girl. He catches my eye, winks, and I bounce from the coffee table into his outstretched arms. This would be romantic if I didn't smack my head on the blasted mirror ball, rather spoiling the effect.

He swings my feet on to the floor and kisses me hello. I gabble introductions to the people around us, who are too drunk to hear what I'm saying, and then we slink off to my bedroom for a close and personal catch-up.

The heavy door of my bedroom muffles the music. My eardrums are ringing; it is nice to grab some peace and quiet, away from the chaos, for a moment.

'You look beautiful,' Tyler tells me suddenly, as I lock the bedroom door on the party. 'You look like an angel.'

Wow, I wasn't expecting that. To my horror, my eyes well up with tears. Bugger, where did this emotion come from? I'm just so unused to gentle compliments. And now I don't know how to respond. Shaking my head, to dislodge the tears before he sees, I revert to what I know best, pushing him on to the bed and straddling him. He kisses me, and I automatically relax, back in my comfort zone. However, just as our kiss is beginning to deepen, his mobile phone trills from his pocket.

He checks the caller ID and says lightly: 'I better get this, baby.'

Clicking open the mouthpiece, he drawls into the receiver: 'All right, babe.' He pauses to listen. 'No, I'm out with the boys tonight, just at the pub. But I won't be too late. I'll see you at home.'

He ends the call, pushes the phone back into his pocket, and then places both hands back up my skirt and on to my arse, as if nothing has happened.

'Sorry,' he says, answering my question before I have a chance to ask. 'That was my fiancée.'

Chapter Five

I wish I could say I kicked him out of the house, but I didn't. My ears plugged with desperation, I pretended not to hear, carried on and let him stay. Because I know nothing, not even jealousy and deception, hurts as much as being lonely. And it's official: I am lonely. So much so and so unrelentingly, that the strength of the emotion distracts me twenty-four hours a day. Though I'm grateful for Eoghan, my guardian angel, watching over me, an immaterial husband is not enough. I want to be taken care of – physically. I want to be looked after again.

If I were mugged in the street tomorrow, who would be angry? Who would go after them? Who would pick me up and carry me home? My friends are wonderful, but there's only so much security a group of girls can provide. I don't want to fight my own battles any more. I want to be protected in the way Eoghan used to protect me.

24 January 2006

Eoghan and I had been dating for what can only have been three weeks, when I was robbed. I was staying in a hostel at the time, sharing a room with four other girls who I didn't know very well. It was a short-term arrangement. I had found a camper van I wanted to buy and was exchanging cash for the keys the next day. I'd arranged to meet the owner of the van, and had taken Aus $1,500 in cash out of my bank account that afternoon. Looking back, somebody must have seen me and followed me, as when Eoghan dropped me back at the hostel at 11 p.m. after our date that evening, the metal security bars had been unceremoniously pulled from the window, the glass smashed, and the bedroom door left ajar.

My suitcase lay in the middle of the floor, still padlocked shut but split down the centre with a Stanley knife. My clothes were strewn across the room: my jewellery – plastic or wooden, and worthless – was scattered across the bed. My diary, where I'd written my most private worries throughout my trip, had been pulled from the inside pocket of my rucksack, the pages ripped out and crumpled into balls. Worse still, photos of my family – my mum, dad and sister – had been torn in half. The Aus $1,500, of course, was gone, along with my bank cards.

'Fuck!' I yell. 'Oh fucking, fucking, fuck.'

Eoghan, who has kept very quiet up until now, surveying the scene, puts his arm around my shoulder and steers me out of the bedroom, on to the balcony that leads back to the main hostel building.

'There's no point standing here and looking at this mess,' he says. 'Come down into the kitchen, and we'll have a cup of tea instead.'

In the deserted, communal kitchen he hands me a cracked mug of sweetened tea, and then grills me on who

I've seen that day: how my roommates have been acting, who I've told about the van I'm buying, if I'd seen anyone suspicious in the bank when I was withdrawing the money.

Shock is setting in and I begin to shiver, my memory blurring. The sofa shakes with the vibration of my shaking legs. Eoghan gets up, goes into the television room next door and comes back with a heap of blankets and a pillow, wrapping me in a comforting cocoon of fabric.

'Right,' he instructs me, 'I'm going to ring the police, but first you need to ring your dad and ask him to cancel your bank cards.'

'Oh no,' I wail. 'I can't. On top of everything, I can't worry him with this now.' The thought of my dad at home recovering from a stem-cell transplant – a brutal treatment used in the last resort – is too much to bear.

'He'll want to know,' Eoghan says simply, and I know he's right. My dad will want to know.

So I take my phone from my handbag and dial the extension for England. My parents – twelve hours behind us, and fast asleep – know I can't be calling with good news.

'I, I, I've been robbed,' I stutter, and burst into tears.

My dad's response surprises me. 'Where's Eoghan?' he asks, quite calmly.

Wiping my eyes on the sleeve of my jumper, I pass the phone obediently to Eoghan. He walks out of the room with it, annoyingly out of my earshot, then comes back twenty minutes later, passing the phone back to me.

'Daddy?' I ask, anxious to see if he's OK.

'It's not the end of the world, pet,' he says, evenly. 'You're safe and that's all that matters. And Eoghan's going to fix the rest.'

I glance at Eoghan, standing above me, who mouths, 'I'll be back in a bit, stay here,' then walks out of the room.

I talk to my dad a while longer, then we say our good-byes, me promising to call him in the morning and to try and get some rest tonight. From the shock of the evening, or the soothing warmth of the blankets still wrapped around me, I'm suddenly overcome with tiredness. I look out of the window, across the courtyard of the hostel, but can't see Eoghan.

I'll just close my eyes for a bit, I think, just for a minute, until he comes back.

Four hours later, I'm woken by Eoghan planting a soft kiss on the end of my nose.

'You all right, Amox?' he asks.

I peer at him through eyes glued shut with sleep: 'Where have you been?'

He unwraps my cocoon of blankets just enough to tuck himself in beside me, wrapping his arms tightly around me. His skin is cold, and when I kiss his shoulder it's salty.

'Have you been on the beach?' I ask.

He looks guilty for a second. 'Only for a bit, just looking for somebody.'

I'm about to interrogate him, but he interrupts me. 'I got you a present, to make you feel better,' he says, handing over a rectangular object wrapped in pages torn from magazines.

Despite myself, I laugh: 'Only you could manage to find me a present at' – I look at my watch – '3.40 in the morning.'

I unwind the makeshift wrapping paper and open the cardboard box inside. Laid within it is the most beautiful diary, with a ruby-red cover decorated with gold stars, the front and back tied with a purple ribbon. 'Where on earth did you find this?' I ask.

He smiles. 'For you, I'd always find a way,' he says.

The next morning, after Eoghan has gone home, I venture back to my bedroom, preparing to face the disarray. But, to my amazement, I find it neat and tidy. Apart from the smashed glass in the window, you wouldn't guess anything untoward had happened.

My clothes are folded in piles under the bed, my jewellery untangled and laid across the duvet. Even the hole in my backpack is pulled across with safety pins.

The photos of my family have been painstakingly Sellotaped back together and left in a pile on my pillow. Placed on top of the pile, however, is a new photograph I haven't seen before. I pick it up, and remember. It was taken the week before, on the sea front, on a particularly scorching day: Eoghan and I, cheeks pressed together, both trying to get our faces in the frame. He has ice cream on his nose; God knows how long it's been there.

I smile, because how could I do anything but?

Months later, Eoghan confesses that, on that evening, as I'd slept, he'd circled the town with a brick in his pocket. Though, of course, he never found the people who did it. The police also had no luck. But I didn't even mind: it didn't matter to me. I had everything I could ever need in him.

It's April and, against my better judgement, I am still dating Tyler. I know, I know, I should know better. The worst thing is that it's not like he is my only option. In the last week, I've been asked on a total of three dates by nice-enough men, all of which I've refused, with no adequate reason. There is nothing wrong with these men, per se, but none of them have blown me away.

Tyler is different. Tyler is proving a remarkable distraction. My relationship with him is so complicated, so webbed with lies and strategies to keep our affair a secret, that I don't have time to mourn Eoghan at all. All thoughts of my husband have been pushed into a corner, because I'm hooked on a whole new soap opera – and Tyler is the star performer. I get the affection of a boyfriend, with the thrill of the chase combined. His fiancée keeps him just out of reach, which is fine with me. I'm all too aware that, this soon after Eoghan, a full-time boyfriend would be too much for me. A time-share boyfriend suits me perfectly. And each day I while away hours plotting how to see him, when to call him, how to orchestrate a secret meeting. For the first time since Eoghan died, I haven't woken every morning wondering about my missing husband and, let me tell you, it's an immense relief. I feel like I've been set free.

It is only a few weeks since I first met Tyler, but we've already fallen into a systematic routine. I don't contact him Sundays or after six o'clock on weekdays. He drives by after work, and I have a beer in hand, waiting. I spend my week's budget on underwear, wear fishnets because he prefers them and don't voice my concern that he won't wear a condom. I have thrown my rulebook out the window. It is ridiculous, of course, to obsess over a man I barely know when I have a husband I should sensibly mourn. But after ten months of missing Eoghan it makes a welcome change. At least this is a man I can fight for.

What's more, Tyler is a man's man. He's big; he's strong; and always ready for a ruckus. I'm safe in the knowledge he'll look after me, fight my battles and shelter me if the sky falls in.

One Friday night, standing outside a pub in Islington with Rachel, one sexed-up punter picks a fight with me. He clumsily tries to grab my arse and, when I protest, says he'll punch my face in. Tyler is drinking at a pub round the corner. I call him and, ten minutes later, he turns up with a 9-iron golf club. He doesn't need to use it: the pure sight of him is enough. That night I know I like him, want him, love him. Well, maybe not love, but something more than indifference, which is what I feel for all those other men.

I know you'll say I'm in denial – my relationship with Tyler is unconventional, I agree – but he really seems to like me. Sometimes when he looks at me, I almost think he loves me.

On Saturday nights, we often all go out together: the three girls and I, and Tyler and his boys. As a rule, he then comes back to mine: we fuck, he leaves by 3 a.m. to get back home, where his fiancée, Hannah, is waiting. This one Saturday, something strange happens. We're in our customary position, me flat on my back, him riding over me. My iPod is singing its way through a hip-hop playlist, and Tyler is gyrating away in time to the fast-paced beats.

But then the track skips – a love song comes on, Damien Rice or someone equally doleful – and the mood in the room changes completely.

The sex has shifted gear as well: it's slower now and softer: closer to lovemaking than the juddering fucking I'm used to with him. Something wet falls on to my cheek. Then – there – another droplet! My eye line, previously fixed somewhere high on the curtain rail, moves to Tyler's face and then, shit, I quickly look away. He's crying. There's no mistaking it. He's actually crying, with real tears rolling down his nose and dropping from his cheek on to mine.

Should I pretend not to see? I look again, and he catches me, our eyes locking. He knows I've seen, but neither of us says anything. I reach up, wrap my arm around his neck, and pull him down to kiss me, strategically shielding his face and the tears from view. And when he comes he whispers what his hormones tell him: 'I love you, Amy. I love you.'

May 2007

I don't often think about the good times I had with Eoghan. It is easier to dwell on the bad times somehow and try to block out just how wonderful he was so that I'll miss him less. But sometimes it's unavoidable and of its own accord my memory will take me back to a place, a conversation, a smell, that reminds me I once had the most brave and caring man alive – if only for a short time.

There is one particular memory that I keep warm inside my heart; locked up tight in a sparkling golden box. Only I have the key. Nobody else shares this memory with me. It was some time between Eoghan's terminal prognosis and our wedding. I can't be more exact, I'm afraid; those weeks all seemed to blur into one as I sleepwalked through them, shell-shocked.

Eoghan was an inpatient for ten days, which was the longest he'd been away from home, and we were both feeling the strain; missing the comfort of each other's company. Visiting times were officially 6 p.m. until 8 p.m. but, as Eoghan had his own room, the nurse let me come and go throughout the day, so I'd drive to the hospital at 7 a.m., through the rush-hour traffic of Dublin city, and not leave until almost 11 p.m., getting back to our empty house after midnight. Needless to say, I was exhausted; my eyes were rimmed black and my complexion had taken on a yellowish tint. I was thankful my parents were back in England and weren't here to see the state of me – although, by this point, Eoghan looked far worse than I did: his face was swollen from the steroids, his head completely bald and his cheeks translucently pale, never a hint of colour in his cheeks. Yet, when I walked into his room each morning, his face lit up with joy – and I'd see the old Eoghan, healthy and well, dancing deep within the pupils of his eyes.

Each day, when the doctor did his morning rounds, we'd look at him beseechingly and ask: 'Can he maybe go home tomorrow?' but Eoghan's blood counts were too low, so it just wasn't safe to discharge him.

On the ninth evening of his stay, as I pack my bag to leave, Eoghan grabs my hand.

'Please, Moxy,' he pleads, his eyes wide and frightened, 'please don't go, I hate it here at night on my own.'

I try to free my hand, but his grip only tightens.

'Eogh, you know I'd love to stay with you, but I can't.'
I stroke his bald head, where the hair is growing back as
a baby-soft down. 'I'm not allowed. It's against the rules.'

'Please, Moxy.' I'm shocked by how young he suddenly
seems. I can't leave him on his own tonight.

'Move over then, Eoghs,' I say, sliding on to the single
bed next to him and curling my body around his so we
both fit on the slim strip of mattress. 'It looks like I'm
sleeping here tonight.'

Lying there, with my head on Eoghan's chest, his thin
arms wrapped around me and a sheet pulled up over my
face in an attempt to hide me from the nurses, we pretend
we're back in our camper van, in Australia, remembering
a time that feels like a lifetime ago.

'Tell me a story,' Eoghan says. This was our favourite
game back then. We had no television to entertain us and
would spend quiet nights in the middle of nowhere,
making up fairytales that mirrored our dreams for the
future.

'There once was a beautiful English princess,' I begin,
'who met and fell in love with an Irish traveller, who'd
come to her castle to sell golden trinkets. The Irishman
asked her to marry him and, although she was due to
marry a handsome prince from the next kingdom, she
chose the traveller, because his wit and optimism were
more attractive then any fortune. Simply, she found the
Irishman spellbinding.

'But the prince from the next kingdom was enraged to
be rejected so sent his army to tear apart the kingdom and
kidnap the princess. The princess hid under her bed, and
the dim-witted soldiers couldn't find her. But the Irishman

was hurt in the battle and by the time the princess found him he was dying.

'"I love you," she told him. "Remember, I'll be with you again one day."

'The princess bent over to kiss her lover goodbye but, as her tears dropped into his wounds, they miraculously healed, the cuts disappearing before her eyes. The Irishman's eyes opened – he was alive and well. And they lived happily ever after, surfing and laughing and doing everything they'd dreamed of. Because that, Eoghan Molloy, is the power of love.'

By the time I finish the story, Eoghan is snoring lightly. I glance up at his face. His forehead is furrowed with pain, even in sleep. I wish I could take the pain away. Tears roll down my cheek and drop on to his chest, and I pray for my teardrops to heal him.

I glance at the door as a nurse stops outside and peers through the glass peephole. She spots me, smiles faintly, and moves on. Nobody disturbs us that night. They know we don't have much time left.

I curl up next to Tyler on my bed, during one of our secret meetings, my nose tucked into the nook of his neck and his arms circling me tightly. I can't remember the last time I felt such strength around me.

We haven't talked about the night he cried, and he hasn't said the L-word since. At the time, I glossed over it, coughed to cover the silence, leapt up from the bed and, flustered, dashed out to the bathroom. By the time I came back into the bedroom, his face was wiped dry, and neither of us has mentioned the incident since.

Today, he asks: 'Do you tell people I'm your boyfriend?'

I am sceptical of this question, unsure of the answer he wants to hear.

I take the safe option and reverse the interrogation: 'Are you happy for me to say that?'

'Are *you* happy to say that?' he copycats back.

'I'm more than happy to call you my boyfriend,' I reply, and then add as an afterthought, 'if that's OK with you.'

He pauses. My stomach drops into my shoes. My face is still buried, so I'm blind to his expression. Finally, thank goodness, I feel his face stretch into a smile. 'Hell, yes,' he says.

So, apparently, now I have a boyfriend: a boyfriend with a fiancée. As if my life weren't farcical enough.

My day's timetable now revolves around the hope I might see Tyler. He's all I think about, all I focus on. It doesn't help that the magazine I have been working for – the exciting new fashion glossy that was due to launch in a few weeks' time – just lost its main investor and flopped, leaving me firmly out of a job and back working from home as a freelancer. Most of my media contacts are based in Ireland – people I met when I worked at a fashion magazine in Dublin – and with no editors recognizing my name in London, I'm a struggling freelancer at that. I'm stupidly bored, with too much time on my hands, and Tyler's plentiful text messages cheer me up no end. I'm reliant on them, and get worryingly antsy if I go half an hour without hearing from him.

Every day I want to see him. Every afternoon I ask him to come over later. This is easier said than done when he has a fiancée to get home to: a suspicious fiancée these days, since she found a smudge of glittery lipgloss on his neck last Friday. He talked his way out of it – God only knows how – but is being a little more careful as a result.

I have probed him about Hannah, his fiancée. He tells me he loves her but isn't in love with her. I know: it's a lazy cliché. He says she's his best friend, but they haven't had sex in six months and he no longer finds her sexually desirable. He says he finds it repulsive to think of having sex with her – I thought that was going a little too far.

I ask why he stays with her, and he says the relationship won't last much longer, but he wants it to run its natural course rather then dumping her and hurting her more.

I've had heart to hearts with enough distressed mistresses in my time to have heard these lines before. I always thought: how can you be so foolish? How can you fall for this bullshit?

I truly never thought I'd be a mistress. I thought my morals were too high, my family too conservative. The 'other woman', a role reserved for those with low self-esteem and rock-bottom self-worth – and yet it fits me like a glove: I know I wear it well. I justify this affair because it suits me right now. And my parents? They know, in uncensored detail, but still no one dares tell the widow she's wrong.

One evening, as the front door slams behind Tyler and I slump on to the sofa, feeling strangely weary, Rachel asks: 'Ame, I don't mean to sound harsh, but you look shattered. Are you sure you can handle this relationship with Tyler? Don't get me wrong, I love the guy. You know I think he's hilarious – as someone to party with. I mean, when we all go out together we have a great time. But as a boyfriend? That's a different story, Ames, and I really don't want to see you get hurt.'

I instantly bristle, but Rachel's my best friend so I force myself to take on board what she's saying.

'I know where you're coming from, Rach, but I can handle him. In fact' – I'm warming to my theme now – 'it's really the perfect situation for me. I don't want the burden of a full-time boyfriend. I'm certainly not ready to fall in love again.'

Rachel nods, but looks sceptical. 'You are falling for him though?' she asks.

'No,' I say. 'How could I? He's so wrong for me. He has a fiancée, for one thing, and he's crass and has got no manners. I could never fall in love with someone like him.'

I'm relieved I can still convince myself of this, but reiterate the words anyway – just to be on the safe side.

'It is perfect, Rachel, because I could never grow too attached to Tyler. I know he's only mine on a time-share. We have a great time together and, then, when he goes home to Hannah, I get time on my own, to spend with my husband. It's an arrangement that suits all of us.'

'Apart from Hannah,' Rachel dares, quietly.

I don't have a response for that.

Tyler knows about Eoghan. Very early on he found a photograph of us together, asked who it was, and I was too slow to lie. Funnily enough, he took it rather well, and it hasn't altered our relationship an inch – much to my relief. But then who is Tyler to judge when he matches me baggage for baggage? A fiancée for a husband: dead or alive, they both bring their complications.

In that sense, who am I to judge Tyler for his adultery?

We're both cheating on our spouses; having sex with other people when we'd promised to be faithful. I can't claim the higher ground. In that sense we surely deserve each other.

On Tuesday night, Tyler is due round at six o'clock. I wait poised in my bedroom in crotchless knickers and suspenders. Neither item is comfortable or functional, but I hope his reaction will be worth it. I want to please him. I want him to need me as much as I need him.

At 6.45, I start to get restless. At 7.15, I'm getting annoyed. At 7.30, my phone beeps with a message.

'I've got to pick up Hannah,' it reads. 'What can I do? I'm sorry, my sweet.'

I volley the phone against my wall in frustration. Unrewardingly, it hits the floor in one piece, doesn't smash into bits as it would on TV. How unsatisfying this evening is proving.

I drag off my stockings, nails ripping through the nylon. The cheap, scratchy knickers get balled into a bottom drawer: out of sight and out of mind. I pull on my comfiest M&S boy shorts and a pair of fleecy pink ankle socks. Then my pyjamas, bobbled with wear, but bought by my mum and so reminiscent of home. I grab a baby wipe and swab the make-up from my face. Instantly, I feel cleansed. I feel safe, and of a sensible mind. Now I can trust myself to reply.

'Fine,' I type, crossing my fingers to lie. 'I really don't mind, Ty. I've got lots of assignments coming up, so won't have time to meet up for a few weeks, but I'll call you sometime soon.'

This is so unlike me he responds instantly: 'Are you OK?'

'Yes.'

'Amy, I've fallen in love with you.'

There it is again. I had wondered how long it would be.

My phone rings, but I transfer the call to voicemail. A moment later I dial my voicemail to listen to the message he's left.

'I have, Amy. I've fallen in love with you.'

'I love you too,' I text, mouthing the words as I write them.

Except all I can think is how lonely I am.

I know I don't love him, even as I tell him. My feelings for Tyler don't even come close. But it feels desperately good to feel those words on my lips. I remember the last time I said them. It feels like a lifetime ago.

2 *July 2007, 6.15 a.m.*

Eoghan and I awoke that morning with our bodies spooned, in our own bed, in our own home. We finished the day in different worlds. I drove back home a widow, my husband no more than a memory.

I'll tell you honestly, I never thought Eoghan would die that day.

On 2 July our alarm sounds as the sun comes up. We have a morning check-up at the hospital: just run-of-the-mill blood tests that will take no more than an hour or two.

When Eoghan wakes, granted, he seems a little confused, but this is nothing unusual. I assume his bloods are slightly low: it is nothing a platelet transfusion can't rectify.

But within half an hour he has visibly deteriorated. His speech is slurred and his eyes unfocused. Looking back, I have no idea how I get him to the car. The path between our house and drive is treacherous at the best of times, with crazy paving leading down a hilled lawn. Today I take the full weight of Eoghan on me.

The drive to the hospital takes almost an hour. I steer with one hand on the wheel and one on Eoghan's shoulder, holding him upright in his seat as his limp body sways with the curves of the road. He seems wonderfully oblivious to his state. He sings softly along to the radio, tapping his foot to an unfathomable beat. I pray he will never realize.

We swerve into the drop-off zone outside the hospital.

'Eoghan, it might be easier if I get you a wheelchair.' I force a smile, not wanting to alarm him. 'Just because you're tired. We might as well abuse the facilities.'

'OK,' he answers lightly.

I leave him in the passenger seat, strapped tightly into the seatbelt. As an afterthought, I lock him into the car. As I walk away, I make sure my steps are slow and measured until I'm out of his range of vision. Then I run: I run for his life.

The oncology department at the Mater Hospital is on the fourth floor. I vault the stairs two at a time, my legs pulsing with adrenaline. As I round the corner of the outpatients ward, I run chest-first into a nurse who knows us well. My face must give everything away.

'Where is he?' she asks sharply.

'He's in the car. He woke up really confused and now . . .' I peter off, suddenly desperately tired: 'Now, I don't know.'

With the help of three nurses and a wheelchair, we collect Eoghan from the car and put him into a bed on the outpatients ward. As soon as his head hits the pillow he dozes into a deep sleep.

'It's OK, Eogh,' I tell him, though he's out for the count and can't hear me. 'Your blood counts have probably dropped, but they'll give you a transfusion, then I'll take you home and we can pack for our trip.'

We are due to fly to London the next day. After much paperwork, dodging of red tape, and many begging phone calls, I'd managed to secure financing from the Irish medical board to take Eoghan to the Royal Marsden Hospital in Fulham for a second opinion. It would be his last chance. My hope was they'd accept him on to one of their medical trials. I never did remember to cancel that appointment.

The nurse hooks Eoghan up to an IV drip of saline, then leaves us alone. As the door thuds softly behind her, Eoghan opens his eyes, smiles and blows me a kiss. It is the first time that day he has recognized my face, and my stomach flutters with a last dash of hope.

'You go to sleep now, baby,' I tell him, taking his hand. 'You're just tired. I'll be right here when you wake up.'

I reach into my bag and pull out his beloved iPod, a Christmas present from my mum and dad the year before. I prop the headphones over his ears and select the playlist he made for our wedding day: an odd mixture of disco tunes and love songs that were the bizarre soundtrack to the proceedings. In the silence of the room the lyrics to 'Masterplan' by Oasis echo from the headphones.

On our wedding day, we'd entered the dining room to this song – on Eoghan's instruction. Our guests had risen from their chairs in a standing ovation. I think they were relieved the groom had made it to the altar at all.

Today, as the song hits its crescendo, Eoghan speaks for the last time. 'Oasis rock,' he says, and laughs. I never hear his voice again. Minutes later, he falls into a coma.

Chapter Six

I am gorging on chocolate at 7.10 a.m. This can only mean one thing: I am back in mourning, with the puffy eyes and sweet tooth that accompany my routine of grief. But this time, for the first time, I'm not mourning Eoghan. After many tears, much soul-searching and a lot of tough love from my housemates, we are all in agreement: the affair with Tyler has to end.

Just four weeks after it all began, I have crossed that invisible line. What started out as a laugh has blossomed into something deeper and altogether more worrying. Certainly not love – I don't even *like* Tyler most of the time – but a complete and illogical dependency. I crave contact with him, even if only to yell at him; whereas he, primarily, depends on his fiancée, and the thought of him going home to her, kissing her, cuddling her and one day marrying her makes me nauseous.

He still says that he loves me, oddly enough particularly when drunk, but I now wish he'd keep his mouth shut. It's an unsavoury relationship, no matter how you dress it up with over-the-top declarations of love. I know I'm the one getting hurt. He seems to have an amazing ability to switch this 'love' on and off, of transferring his affection to the woman he's with at the time, whoever is nearest – Hannah or me. In short, I don't think he really minds.

I switch on my computer and send an email to my mother. I know if I put my plans in writing, I'll be forced to have the courage of my convictions later.

amoxmolloy@gmail.com
Sent: Mon 31/03/2008 7:19
To: Mum
You'll be overjoyed to hear I'm going to end it with the Tyler.

    I'm going to give him an ultimatum: me or her. And before you roll your eyes, I'm not even considering the fact he'll say yes. He doesn't have the guts to end the relationship with her. Why would he? He's got two doting girls, he's living the dream. No, I need to give him an ultimatum to give myself a good hard reality check. I need to cut myself loose, and I know I don't have the willpower to do it unless I shock myself into seeing he'll never choose me.

    I know it's stupid, especially for me, being a widow and all, and with the fickle way I've worked my way through men before, but I really feel sad about this one, Mum.

    I don't want Eoghan to be the only man in my life again. I need more than him. I thought my skin was tougher than this, after everything I've survived. I don't want to go back to being lonely, Mummy.

    With love from your bewildered daughter. Amy. x

ccollins@aol.co.uk
Sent: Mon 31/03/2008 8:03
To: amoxmolloy@gmail.com
I knew that you were not right, even before you
sent me this. On Saturday, when you phoned me, I
knew he was getting under your skin. That is why
I changed the subject when you kept bringing the
conversation to him.

Amy, I am so proud of you and the young
woman you've turned into. In that last year, how
you handled Eoghan, good God, you don't need to
do any more in my eyes, you've outdone all my
expectations. And I've listened to you talk about
Tyler and held my tongue. But, come on now,
you're a smart girl. Don't let this go on any more.
If he is prepared to cheat on his fiancée now, he
will, without doubt, do the same to you.

I know I am being hard, but it is because I don't
want you to get hurt. I would rather you got hurt
now than further down the line when you come to
rely on him even more. I do understand that you
don't want to be lonely, but, with those girls
around you, your career and the person that I
know you are, I am positive it won't be long before
you find someone who is prepared to give you 100
per cent. They won't be Eoghan – no one can be
that beautiful man – but they will be good for you
in different ways. Tyler is not.

You need to be very aware that you are still very
vulnerable and that you are looking for someone to

take care of you. I don't give a shit what Tyler needs. All I know is that you are still recovering from a shattering experience and the last thing you need is to get emotionally involved in a triangle of deceit that will leave you more scarred than you already are.

Don't think for one moment that I don't understand, because no one loves you like I do. It's because I love you so much that I will give you tough questions to ask yourself.

I will end now as I am starting to cry; I think it's my hormones. I cannot bear to think of you being sad.

Love you
Mum

I stare at this email for longer then necessary. It's been a long time since my mum has given me an uncensored opinion, so scared is she to rock my already unsteady boat and upset me. I know, for her to say this, she must really hate Tyler. And I know, sensibly, that everything she's written is true. I need to walk away, so why is it so hard to do?

Before I have a chance to gather my thoughts my mobile beeps.

'Are you OK, my sweet?' the text from him reads.

Now, usually, I work hard to project the image of a fun-time girl; I always plaster on a smile and pretend I'm on top of the world. But today I don't have the energy.

'For once, not really. I'm not doing this any more,' I

text back, bracing myself for what I know will lead to an argument that lasts for days. Tyler isn't used to not getting his own way.

Forty minutes and two sugary mugs of caffeine later, I am ready to compose a text. 'I hate to say this Ty,' I write, 'but I've fallen for you, and it's messing with my head to share you. You need to think: her or me?' SEND.

His reply lands in my inbox within seconds, but it takes me ten more minutes to muster up the courage to open it. 'I'm coming over after work. See you at six, my sweet,' it reads.

I spend the remaining day in a state of unrest. By the time he arrives I have changed my outfit a total of seven times. Normally, when Tyler drops by, I dress for sex, in clothing chosen for easy access and seduction, but today I need to give out a different message entirely. Today, I want to show vulnerability. I want him to see me as a girlfriend, not just a sex toy, and this involves a whole new marketing strategy. I decide on a plain white vest top, loose cut and Miss Sixty jeans, and curl my blond hair into loose, falling ringlets. It's the perfect medley of fashion and defencelessness.

When Tyler arrives, he looks unusually edgy. He knows he can't say what I'm desperate to hear.

'So?' I start lamely.

'So, what changed?' he asks.

I relay the little white lie I have rehearsed: 'I had some bad news yesterday, and all I wanted to do was call you, but I couldn't because it was after six and you were with your fiancée.' I figured this elaborate tale might justify my abrupt change of heart. 'It made me realize I need more.

I need someone who can be there for me, take care of me. I don't want to share you any more.'

He sits heavily on the stool of my dressing table. He looks defeated. When I realize he isn't going to speak any time soon, I continue my monologue. But I'm losing my momentum now. I wish I could look at the notebook where I've written this whole speech down.

'Tyler, I don't want to share you. I know we've never really talked about you leaving Hannah for me, but now I want you to. And I appreciate it's not something you can do overnight, but I need to be reassured that it's at least where we're headed.'

I sit cross-legged on the bed in front of him. He's perched awkwardly on the edge of the stool, his bulk far too big for such a dainty piece of furniture. As he shuffles uncomfortably, it lets out a creak, and I wonder if the wooden legs might cave. Any other time this would be quite comical, but this is no time for jokes. Our gaze is locked in each other's pupils.

'It is something I'd consider in the future, Ame' – my heart leaps – 'but not now.' My heart thuds to my feet.

Tyler continues: 'My relationship with Hannah is rocky, but I do still love her. I've told you that over and over. She's always been loyal to me, and she's never actually done anything wrong. I owe her.'

Then he utters five words that make my blood boil: 'You need to chill out.'

I jump off the bed, spin on my heels and slam out the door, stamping down the stairs to the basement, as this seems the nearest escape route to hand. Rachel looks up from the sofa as I storm down the stairs like a cyclone. 'I am going to kill him,' I snarl.

'So, it's not going well,' she replies: more statement than question.

I don't answer but walk to the five spirit optics which stand like soldiers on the kitchen window sill, pour a measure of vodka, shoot it then repeat: 'I'm going to kill the bastard.'

Instead, I about-turn to my bedroom and shag him.

I know, it's appalling, but in my defence, that thin line between love and hate really is a fine one. And, truthfully, as I walk back into the room, I have every intention of chucking him out there and then. But as I stand there, so angry, my heart thudding out of my chest and goosebumps prickling through my skin, I think, Jesus, something about this feels fantastic.

For months before and after Eoghan died I felt completely numb. My body shut down, it just hibernated. I'd sit on the sofa for hours, staring into space, and hours would pass by without me knowing or caring. I couldn't be bothered to talk, eat or move, but I wasn't actually sad per se, I just didn't feel any more.

'I'm fine,' I'd tell people, and I was just that. Just 'fine'. Mediocracy was my middle name. And that was the problem: I never felt happy, I never felt sad, I had simply hit a stalemate, suspended between emotions, feeling nothing. A doctor might have called it depression, I suppose.

I'd test myself sometimes, to see if I could drum up any emotion. I'd watch my wedding video, start to finish, or play a song from our wedding day, or look through

Eoghan's mobile phone, filled with archived texts from me professing how much I loved him. I'd desperately try to squeeze out a tear, but I couldn't. I'd used up my quota of emotions.

I was beginning to worry I'd be numb for ever.

Then I met Tyler. And, even when he insults me, disappoints me and lets me down, at least then I can hate him. At least then I feel something. Even hatred is better than nothing. And when I'm full of fire and anger, when I have my mind set on the goal of getting Tyler, at least I have a purpose, at least there's some point to being alive.

Chapter Seven

Nothing's changed between Tyler and me since I tried and failed to dump him. Our affair continues through the next two weeks, with neither of us ever mentioning the argument, glossing over the little hiccup like it never happened, and I become resigned to continuing our relationship; I can't bring myself to end it just yet. Anyway, he treats me well enough, compliments me, and takes me out for a drink every once in a while, when Hannah's working late. I start to wonder if maybe I'm being too picky. Aren't we all meant to have one true love, only one? Well, I had my chance with Eoghan, and I let him down, I let him go. I don't deserve a second go.

The age of true romance is gone anyway – in the twenty-first century people just don't court each other that way. In this day and age flowers are more likely a sign of guilt than graciousness, love letters have lost out to emails – and has any modern man ever serenaded a woman when sober? I have to face facts: there are no Romeos left. I need to be thankful for what I can get.

I focus on this theory as I stare at the text message my 'boyfriend' has just sent me. Reading it again, it seems Tyler is ready to take 'us' to the next level of intimacy.

For the first few weeks of our fling, Tyler was on his best behaviour – attentive and sweet and really rather lovely – but I've noticed something shifting lately. Ever since I gave him the ultimatum and asked him to leave Hannah for me, the sex is getting rougher and his requests in the bedroom more erratic. He's realized he has power over me, so he's testing me, seeing how far he can push me. And this text message just proves it. He's obviously done with the niceties: 'Do you love me, my sweet? Will you wee in my mouth?' it reads.

Now, I'm no prude but this crosses a line. 'Eoghan' – I address a patch of air I imagine to be my husband – 'when I said on your deathbed that I'd do everything you dreamt of and never had a chance to do, this wasn't what I had in mind.'

2 *July 2007, 11.50 p.m.*

It is ten to midnight when Eoghan passes away.

The consultant takes me to one side around lunchtime. He makes it very clear; I am not to be deluded.

'This is it, Amy,' he tells me. 'One of two things will happen now. Eoghan may wake from this coma temporarily, but within hours or days will fall back into unconsciousness. Or else he'll remain in this state until the pressure on his brain stops its functioning. Then he'll drift away. It's impossible to know how long, but we do know he won't make a recovery from this.'

It's a relief to hear it at last. I have been waiting for this day since the terminal prognosis in May; I have never let myself dwell on it, but the dread has always lurked in the background, a shadow in my mind, and with every check-up, every doctor's visit, I've been waiting. To hear it is the end. So this is how it feels, I think, to face your darkest fear. I'm surprised; I expected it to be far worse.

'I don't want him to be in any pain,' I say.

'He won't be.' The doctor's tone is reassuring: 'We'll make sure he has everything he needs.'

'And I don't want him to know,' I add. 'If he wakes up beforehand, please don't tell him it's over.'

'That's your choice, Amy,' the doctor replies. 'I'll tell the nurses that's your wish.'

I can't remember who I contact first or how I find the right words, but suddenly people begin to arrive: shell-shocked family and friends coming to say their goodbyes.

I sit on the edge of the hospital bed and tuck Eoghan's head into the crease of my arm. They've moved us into a different room and it's full of people – well over the allowed quota of two visitors – and I think how kind it is of the nurses to make an exception for us. I consider telling some people to come back tomorrow, or to visit us next week when Eoghan's home and more in the humour, but they're here now so may as well stay.

I pin photos of our wedding above the hospital bed, and the conversation drifts to memories of that happy day. It is hard to believe we married nearly four weeks before and I laugh, remembering how, at the reception, Eoghan had out-danced us all. I glance down at him now, wondering if my laughter has woken him. He must be tired, I think, he's out like a light and sleeping so soundly.

Around nine o'clock things take a turn. Eoghan's breath

starts to catch in his throat: it's a sound I've never heard before and I pray I never hear again. I will never forget that noise, a rasping, gasping; the sound of someone drowning, falling under the water then surfacing and struggling for air. Somebody runs for a nurse, but when she comes to check his vital signs we're told there's nothing to be done.

'Do something.' I grab her arm. 'He needs help. Listen to him.'

But, unlike me, she knows this sound and has heard it before, many times. This is the sound a man makes as he dies.

The nurse adjusts the oxygen tube that forks into his nostrils, more to appease me than because it will make any difference, and leaves the room. Now our group falls silent. I clutch Eoghan's hand and stare fervently at the bedsheet. I've felt so strong until this moment and so sure that I can cope. Again, he inhales: rasps, coughs and splutters. His head jumps from my arm with the force and then falls back into the mound of pillows. How will I feel when he takes his last breath, when this noise that terrifies me so much is replaced with silence? Will that prove more terrifying still?

'I can't do this,' I cry and break for the door. I need to get out. I need not to hear.

I sprint down the corridor and swing left into the patients' toilets. I grasp the side of the basins with sweating hands and stare into the mirror at my ashen face. This person doesn't look like me. This moment doesn't feel even slightly real.

My phone rings in my pocket; my dad's mobile number is flashing on the screen.

My parents are en route; they had booked flights on the first plane from London after I called them this morning.

'Where are you?' I shout hysterically into the phone. 'Daddy, he's dying. Where the fucking hell are you two?'

My poor father's heart must have broken: 'Our flight was delayed, we're in Dublin airport. Amy, we're on our way.' His speech is splintered.

'I can't do this,' I stammer; he won't have the answers but I have to ask: 'How can I sit through that moment, Daddy? How am I meant to say goodbye to him?'

'I don't know,' he replies helplessly. 'But, Amy, you love him, so you don't have a choice.'

I hang up, take a final deep breath, push open the bathroom door and step back into the hospital corridor. I look right in the direction of Eoghan's room and see two of his friends sprinting towards me. They seem to move in slow motion. I see their mouths open and bellow an exclamation, but I can't hear them. I don't need to hear them to know.

As I run through the door of the private room the sight of Eoghan hits me like a brick wall. His cheeks are blue. His lips are purple. He's dead, I think, and I wasn't there. My knees give way and I crumple to the floor. Then I hear him take a breath from nowhere. A nurse steps forward to help me up but I have already ricocheted to my feet and crossed to Eoghan's side.

I press my cheek against his face. Already his body smells like a stranger's. The skin I've stroked so many times feels different: cooler, tougher now. His breathing is slowing down. The gap between each gasp is lengthening. I want it to be over for him. I want him to be free of this.

'You can go now, Eoghan,' I whisper in his ear. My instincts say he's holding on too long. 'You haven't let me down. We did everything we could, my baby. You did everything you promised me you would.'

I repeat words we've said a thousand times: 'I love you, Eoghan, that's never going to change. And I'll be with you again one day. I'll meet you again on the beach at Byron Bay, just like we promised. I'll meet you again on the beach at Byron Bay and, until then, I'll do everything we planned, for the both of us.'

I press my lips against his ear and will him to hear me: 'Please go now, baby. It's OK; it's time for you to leave me.'

His chest falls, his breath stops.

I rest my cheek on Eoghan's chest and close my eyes. I am vaguely aware of the room filling up around me, with people, grief and noise. Crying, weeping; it doesn't sound human.

'Amy, your parents are here,' someone says, and my father is next to me. He places his hand on the small of my shivering back. He doesn't speak. What words are there to say? This isn't a bruised knee, or a lost doll. His youngest daughter has been widowed. And he fears there is no way of fixing this, possibly ever.

My mum follows my father into the room, and in front of her is Eoghan's body, his face already yellowing as the blood drains away. She loves him like a son, and she'll mourn him like a son, even though she doesn't yet realize. 'My lovely man,' she whispers, pushing through his friends and leaning to kiss his cheeks: 'My lovely, lovely man.'

* * *

Months later, sitting in my parents' living room, I ask my mother if she regrets the fact they weren't there in time to say goodbye.

'But we did,' my mum replies, and my father, standing behind her, nods in agreement.

'But when?' I ask. 'You didn't make it to the hospital in time. And how, when Eoghan didn't believe he was dying? Did he tell you, Daddy' – I'm scared now, of what awful admission may have been hidden from me – 'did he tell you he was scared? Did he tell you he was dying? Did he know deep down and not tell me?'

'No, Ame,' my father says, looking me squarely in the eyes. 'I swear he never said anything like that to me. He was planning your future, right until the end: buying a house, having children, he was expecting to spend a lifetime with you.'

I believe him, because, since my widowdom, my father doesn't hide the truth from me, and because Eoghan and my father's relationship, built on shared experiences and total unbridled honesty, was more blood than in-laws. I know if Eoghan had doubts, he would have gone to him.

'So,' I say, remembering my thread, 'when did you say goodbye to him?'

My mother reaches subconsciously to touch the crucifix that hangs from a silver thread around her neck, willing it to strengthen her.

'After your wedding,' she begins. 'We came to your honeymoon suite to say goodbye, because we were flying back to London. But it was more than that.'

'You knew?' I ask.

'Yes,' she says, so quietly I almost don't hear her. But even if she hadn't spoken I already knew the answer.

'And you?' I ask my father.

'Yes,' he replies. 'I knew, in my gut, that would be the last time we'd see him.'

Until then I'd forgotten that moment. It had seemed so insignificant, and my brain was so inundated with worries that year, I simply didn't have space to file all my memories as well. But now I remember it well: the last time I saw the three people I love the most in the same room, my mother cupping my husband's cheeks with both hands and kissing his face, again and again.

It was two days after my wedding – my parents had stayed a day longer than the other guests. I wonder if they wanted more time with him. I wonder if they knew, that months and even years on, they'd need to have had that one last day.

Eoghan is dressed in the hotel's complimentary bathrobe, a size too large and girlishly white and fluffy, teamed with a scarlet bandana and matching red Converse trainers. The eyepatch he's been forced to wear since the tumour in his brain started to affect his eyesight sits crookedly over his right eye. He looks quite absurd but also wonderfully, illogically, beautiful.

He's excited, having just come back from a swim in the hotel pool, where I was teaching him to spin an underwater somersault. His cheeks are flushed pink, and his skin gleams from the E45 cream I've just slathered over him. He hops from one foot to the other, and though his limp arms and bowed shoulders give away the fact that his body is tired, his zest and charisma still fill the room. It is quite impossible to take your eyes off him. He has 'it' – even after multiple rounds of chemo, with just weeks until his death, he still possessed that magical 'it'. I'm sorry, I wish I could find a word to explain this to you, but every noun I test out doesn't come close. The consonants aren't bold enough, the vowels are lacking spark. No noun, no adjective could describe him, but all his friends and family knew our lives would be colourless without him.

My mother felt this, more than most, and yet she had to say goodbye. I remember her tears. I wonder how I didn't see this was the last goodbye.

'I'll be seeing you in a few weeks, Carmel,' Eoghan was telling my mother – we'd planned to fly to England for a visit in July. 'Make sure you've got that bacon I like. Me and Steve will be needing a fried brekkie.'

My mother smiled. You just couldn't help it when face to face with him.

'I will, Owney,' she said and pulled him into a hug, wrapping him, her knuckles white as she clutched his shoulders.

'But, until then, you need to promise me something.'

'Anything for my favourite mother-in-law.'

'Just remember how much we love you, Owney,' she says, using the affectionate pet name he loved her calling him. 'Promise me, you remember how much we love you, always.'

Holding him at arm's length now, I see her scan his face, trying desperately to memorize every wisp of hair and crease of skin. She reaches out to place the palm of her hand on his chest, feeling his heart beat strongly, spurred by love for her daughter.

'You're part of our family now, Owney,' she says, speaking only for him, oblivious to my father and me in the room. 'And we're joined by a golden thread between our hearts. Right here.' She touches her chest and then his own. 'It leads between us all. So no matter where we go or what might happen, we'll always be together.'

Eoghan nods, unusually solemn. 'I won't forget, Carmel,' he tells her.

My mother pulls her hand from his chest, kisses him once more on the cheek and steps back. Her goodbye is finished and she has said all she needs to.

For Eoghan and my father the goodbye is simpler but no less heartfelt. Eoghan, who once told me he had no memory of his own father ever cuddling him, enveloped my father in a bear hug, so close you couldn't see which limbs were which man's.

'I love you, buddy,' Eoghan tells him.

'I love you, Eogh,' my dad replies.

That was their last goodbye and the only thing worth saying.

Fast-forward three weeks, to a hospital room where my mother places her hand, once again, on the chest of her son-in-law. This time his heart doesn't beat under her palm.

'My lovely, lovely man,' she repeats. I doubt she knows she's said it aloud.

I feel like my skin is about to burst. An odd feeling is engulfing me. I'll grow to know it as grief. I'll learn to live with it, but not yet. For now my body can't cope with this new and all-consuming alien emotion. My skin can't stretch to hold it inside me: I'm shuddering, pulling at the skin around temples with my fingertips. I need to get out, I can't breathe. I catapult from the bed and push through the crowded room, to where I remember there once was a door. But that's a wall. Get me out of here. I spin on my heels, and the world spins with me, but in the opposite direction, mocking me. Someone grabs my shoulders – my father – but I shrug him off. 'Leave me, I want to be alone,' I plead.

Before he has a chance to argue I see the door, and bolt for it.

I race down five flights of stairs from Oncology, to the ground-floor exit, past the night porter and into the car park, empty apart from one deserted ambulance. I walk to the centre of the car park, a hundred yards from the hospital building and everything it contains, and I stare up at the midnight sky, a pitch-black blanket stained with silver clouds.

I stare up expectantly. I'm waiting to see him, or some vision of him at least, ascending into the atmosphere, but all I can pinpoint are the headlights of airplanes.

'Where are you?' I scream into the emptiness. 'You said you'd never leave me, so where the fuck are you, Eoghan?'

I believed in an afterlife. In the last hard weeks of Eoghan's life, when my resolve had slipped and I'd started to see his end was in sight, I'd at least had faith that if Eoghan died I'd still feel him with me and he'd never truly leave me. But here, tonight, I feel deserted.

An ambulance rushes into the car park with its sirens blaring. Two doctors hurry out of the hospital building and a stretcher is pulled from the rear of the ambulance. A clearly distraught woman – wife, mother, who knows? – stumbles out of the ambulance and falls over her feet to keep up with the patient.

I walk nearer, morbidly intrigued. There's no need really, as she's crying so loudly I can hear her over the sirens from across the car park anyway.

'Please don't let him die. You have to keep him alive.'

A young nurse appears at her side. It's a nurse I recognize from my stints in A&E with Eoghan. She places a supportive arm around the wife and I hear her comfort her with:

'He's going to be fine. He's had a mild heart attack, but he's stable now, so try not to worry.'

By now I'm standing just a few feet away from them, but neither notices. It's my first taste of the invisibility that will descend on me over the coming months. They pass by me, are swallowed into the corridors of the hospital, and the car park is silent again.

I hate that fucking woman, I think: they've had forty years together already and still he's going to live. Bitch. I want to spit out the word, but it falls limply from my lips. I want to hate her but I just don't have it in me.

With the car park providing no comfort, I walk back up to the ward. Eoghan's friends are dotted in pairs along the hospital corridor, from the lift to the private room his body is laid in: they are clutching each other and crying. My father, standing like a watchman at the entrance, spots me, rushes over and tries to hug me, but I dodge his arms. I don't want him to touch me. I don't want anyone near me.

'Come and have a cup of tea,' he says.

I'm led to the nurse's station, positioned next to Eoghan's room. I can just see the end of his bed and his slippered feet through the open doorway. A nurse leads me to a wheeled chair and places a polystyrene cup in my hand. Tea, I think, though when I sip from the cup I can't taste anything. She offers me a china plate of custard creams, as if we're at a tea party, and absent-mindedly I take one, pull the two biscuit halves apart and nibble the icing from the inside, like I used to as a child. A group of people stand round me in a semicircle. I'm not sure who they are or why they are all here, and I think it's rude to ask, isn't it? But why are they looking at me?

I finish the last crumbs of my biscuit, and reach for the plate again. I may as well take another few for the journey. 'Shall we go home now?' I ask Eoghan.

'OK, pet,' my father answers, and I think, how rude, I'm not talking to you.

I drive myself home from the hospital, happy that I didn't get a parking ticket even though, for some reason, I'd left my car in a bus lane. My mum decides to come with me in my Fiat and my dad follows in his hired car. Eoghan must be riding with him, I think.

We're all worn out by the time we get home to Dalkey, not surprising really, as it's half past three. Bugger, I think, sleepily setting my alarm for the morning: I have to wake Eoghan in three hours for his first round of medicine. He'll be grouchy – he always is when he doesn't get a good night's sleep.

I make four cups of tea, set up the sofa bed for my

parents, apologizing for the musky smell it gives off, and get undressed and into my pyjamas. I fluff out the duvet on our double bed, slide under the cold, crisp covers and roll on to the left-hand side, as Eoghan likes to sleep on the right. Just before I fall asleep I remember we're flying to London tomorrow and think, how odd that my parents chose this week to visit.

At 6.15 reality hits me. I sit up in bed and scream and scream. Then everything turns black.

'Do you love me, my sweet? Will you wee in my mouth?'

Tyler seems surprised when I reply to his text with a stout: 'No. No way.'

His reply ricochets back: 'Why not? If you loved me you should.'

My nose wrinkles with disgust: cheap shot, Tyler. Today, I can't be bothered with this, so I turn my phone off.

The next morning, I switch it back on at 7 a.m., expecting a backlog of calls or texts but getting nothing. Muttering motivational mantras under my breath, I quickly write out a text and send it before my heart can protest: 'I'm sorry, I can't do this. I deserve more than a time-share boyfriend. I deserve more than being your personal whore. I've got to end it before I get hurt any more. You know where I am if you ever leave her. Don't contact me. This is how it's got to be.'

I am abjectly disappointed by the response: 'I understand, baby. I am going to miss you. Love you.'

What an anticlimax. Where are the dramatics? Why isn't he fighting for me and trying to change my mind? I can't believe he's just going to let me walk away.

My phone vibrates against my leg: 'I just want to run away with you,' he adds.

Now this is more like it.

By the end of the day I am riding high on adrenaline. Right at home when surrounded by drama, the performer in me is revelling. I am not proud of how I'm acting, but I can't seem to stop myself. Tyler provokes this side of me.

Our messages have progressively got more over the top as the day's gone on. A conversation that began relatively sensibly is now taking on the tones of high tragedy.

'I can't handle not seeing you,' he tells me. 'Life will be empty without you.'

An hour later his declarations get wilder: 'I need to see you!' – his texts are dotted with exclamation marks – 'We're perfect for each other. I love you.'

I feel sick: the melodrama is curdling my stomach, but still I don't stop him; it's so nice to be wanted, and for someone to say they need me, again.

The fraught exchange continues with Tyler issuing more and more elaborate declarations of love, and me sidestepping them, until: 'I love you, Amy. I'd marry you. Please just meet me for a minute.'

With this last revelation, my previous resolve cracks in two. 'OK,' I reply. 'Come over and see me.'

Our two-way conversation ends abruptly, and my mobile's screen dims for the first time since breakfast. His silence is telling.

I text again: 'Do you want to see me then?'

Two hours later, and his belated reply arrives: 'Sorry. I

can't make it today, babes. Taking Hannah out for dinner. Actually, I think it's best we just be friends. I hope you understand, Ames.'

Bastard, I think, checkmate to him. In this round of the dating game, I have definitely been outplayed.

The homemade sign is still stuck on my mirror from months ago, the corners peeling away where the Blu-tack's dried out and forgotten its function. My eyes brush over it every morning, but it's been there so long, it has no significance: the lettering has lost its meaning, becoming another section of the wallpaper's pattern and nothing more.

Today, I stop, stare and take stock. 'Go on dates,' it challenges.

OK, I think, with Tyler AWOL, what reasons have I not to?

That is how I ended up on a date with Sam. Sam, another Irishman, who I met at the gym, when we were sitting side by side in the sauna. He groaned loudly in the heat, I said: 'I know how you feel,' and the conversation rolled from there. Twenty minutes later I asked him for a drink, because what else do I have to lose?

I meet him at the same bar I met Tyler. Odd, I know, but it was his suggestion and not my own. Sam walks through the door, and I'm struck by just how Irish he looks. Not like Eoghan, who after too many years travelling had shed his Dublin fashion sense for an Australian inspired surfer's style, but more like Eoghan's brothers. Unfashionable would be a harsh description, but it's hard to describe the faded jeans and pinstriped shirts, tightly tucked into his belt. Still, I must have an open mind, and as the evening goes on, we get on well, the conversation flows and I start to have hope. He seems like a nice guy, I think this could go somewhere.

Outside the bar he leans in to kiss me goodnight: short enough to be polite, but just long enough to say he would like more, at a later date. He says he's had a great time, and asks to take me out to dinner the following Saturday, to a small and cosy tapas bar, conveniently placed between our houses. 'Of course,' I agree without flinching at the second date invitation. 'That would be lovely.'

The next day I wake up and wonder why my stomach is in knots. Oh, I remember, and a gentle smile curls the corner of my mouth before I realize it.

I lean across the side of the bed and sweep my computer off the floor and into my lap, powering it up and clicking into my inbox, planning to send an email to Rachel, who's already left for work, with news of last night's unexpected success.

My stomach flips with excitement when the first email, sitting stoically at the top of my list, is from him. Keen, I think, he must be as excited as me.

I reach the second line and the blood drains from my face, from my hairline to my feet, like a tide rushing out of me.

Morning, Amy.
    Just googled you and read your article on the Daily Mail website.
    Sounds like you've had a tough year or two.

I can't make Saturday after all. Something's come up, sorry. But I'll give you a call some time.

Sam.

I slam my laptop shut. Stupid fool: who was I kidding, thinking I could be like the rest of them? I can't escape my widowdom. They hear his footsteps, heavy behind me. No matter how fast I move, I can't walk anywhere without his weight heavy on my shoulders.

So I revert to what I know. I email all the girls at work with Sam's email copied and pasted into the body of the text, begging them to agree to a girl's night out, that evening. I need to get drunk: I need to get laid. I've proved that's the only thing I can do right these days.

We meet after work, at our regular haunt, the Living Room, the same place I met Tyler, Sam, and most of the men in my line-up. We go there all too frequently, partly because it's ten minutes from our house, but also because I get free drinks from one of the barmen, Kirk. Since we first came to the bar, when we moved into our house, around eight months ago now, Kirk and I have flirted outrageously, passed suggestive notes across the bar, and pinched each other's body parts as we've crossed each other's path. But, so far, we've never put our money where our mouths are. I'm no fool really, and I'm fully aware he only wants me because he's not yet had me. All barmen are cut from the same cloth. As soon as he's notched me on his bedpost, our handy supply of free drinks will run dry, and the attention he gives me will stop, just like that.

Tonight, as the girls and I sit in a cushioned booth, dissecting the turn of events with Sam, Kirk ambles over to serve us. He lays down three cocktails, of eye-watering strength, and winks at me.

I lift my iced glass, and the napkin he has laid beneath it catches my eye. A sentence is scrawled across it in biro: 'Tonight? I finish at 3.'

I don't look up at the bar, as I know he is watching, but to Lucy, who's sitting beside me, I mumble out of the side of my mouth: 'Look at this,' and nudge the note across to her.

She laughs, and I cringe as she looks up, not too subtly.

'He's watching you, Ame, you'll have to say something back.'

'Who's got a pen?' I ask, and Rachel digs her liquid eyeliner from the depths of her handbag.

I turn the napkin over and dash off a reply.

'What are you writing?' asks Rachel, leaning forward. 'Do you actually want to go through with it? You've always said you don't really fancy him.'

I think of Sam, and his brazen rejection. So I don't really like Kirk – well, that's far easier. At least then I won't be led to disappointment.

The girls are waiting. 'I'm writing our address, of course,' I tell them, and ask a passing waiter to take the note to the bar before I can change my mind.

The girls and I leave the bar at one o'clock, and our doorbell rings at 3.30. When I open the door he's leant against the pillar at the bottom of the steps, smoking a roll-up cigarette, with a baseball cap partly covering his face. I wonder if the stories that he has a girlfriend are true. I wonder if he's heard rumours about me and is wondering the same thing.

He stubs his cigarette out on the grass before climbing the steps to the front door, where he kisses me, as if it's something he's done a hundred times before. He pulls away and says: 'That's something I've wanted to do for weeks.'

'So why didn't you?' I ask, with one eyebrow raised. I'm teasing him now, thinking he's jesting.

'You're an odd one, Amy,' he says. 'All jokes aside, you really don't give anything away. It's almost like you're hiding something, that you only trust those three girls you live with to know.'

I digest this for a moment, thinking how bizarre it is that this stranger, a barman, has summed me up so well. But I can't dwell on it now, and it seems he doesn't want to either, as he kisses me again, and follows me to the bedroom, where one thing leads to the usual.

I wake the next morning as he's stumbling around my bedroom floor searching for his far-flung clothing.

'Are you off?' I ask, always weaker in the morning, looking for reassurance.

'I've got to get to work soon,' he lies, as it's not even 9 a.m. and the bar doesn't open until noon. 'But I'll call you later, I could come round again.'

'All right,' I say, plastering a smile on my face. 'We could meet up for a late drink after you finish your shift.'

I call him at 10 p.m. that evening, then eleven and, finally, resignedly, at midnight. The first two times it rings out, and the third I'm diverted to voicemail.

I can't do this any more: staking out bars, stalking men, selling myself for a free drink and some flattery. I look at what I am and I don't feel proud. I look at where I've come from and I wonder where it all went wrong.

I was a loyal wife once. I was proud of myself and treated myself with respect. Everyone said I was a good girl: how I'd cared for my dad and looked after Eoghan. Now I'm a widow who begs strangers back to my bed of an evening, because, almost a year on, I'm still scared of waking with a big gaping space in my bed that used to be filled up by him.

I kid myself I'm in control. I boast that I've survived so commendably, but who am I kidding? I'm not convinced and neither, in truth, are the people around me. Even the men I meet see right through me.

I wasn't always like this, believe me. When I left for Australia I was enviably self-sufficient and stubbornly independent. I was a solo flier; so much so that when Eoghan and I first met I pushed him away. I saw no function for a boyfriend. I was just fine on my own. But Eoghan persevered and, though it pained me at first to admit it, I fell in love. Now, three years on, I'm not so tough. I'm damaged goods. I'm simply exhausted.

I tried, Eoghan, I really did. But no one told me how gruelling grief is. I'm tired of carrying your dead weight with me. You left me: so leave me totally! I'm walking up a hill as it is, which isn't easy, and the last thing I need is you pulling me back.

I never thought I would be so desperate to escape my husband. I thought we were for ever. I naively believed we could conquer any hurdle, just as long as we were together.

3 April 2007

This is the day I am told the cancer has spread to Eoghan's brain.

He's nine months into chemo at the time, and the side effects are, at this point, surprisingly manageable. His appetite is good, he has lost no more weight and, apart from late-night headaches, which we put down to stress, he never complains. We thought it was going so well. Then, one morning I wake at 6 a.m. to find him out of bed and pacing the length of our newly mowed garden.

I stand in the doorway to the conservatory and call out to him: 'Eoghan, what are you doing? Why are you up so early?'

He turns at the sound of my voice and trips over his feet, taking more than a moment to regain his balance. It's a warm spring morning but suddenly I'm shivering.

He crosses the garden to answer me. 'I'm sure it's nothing,' he says, but his tone betrays him. I can instantly see he is scared. 'It's just, when I woke up this morning, the sight in my right eye was blurred.'

I breathe a sigh of relief. He's overreacting and, 'That could be nothing,' I tell him. 'It's probably just an eye infection. It'll be better in a day or two.'

'I'm going to call the hospital anyway, just to let them know,' he says. He is being over-cautious and I want to tell him to relax, but keep my opinion to myself. This is his cancer and his body after all.

If you're not a private patient, it's impossible to get hold of a consultant before 9 a.m. In theory, there should be a doctor on call, but they are infamously hard to track down. Eoghan leaves three messages and, at 9.15, our liaison nurse phones the house. I walk out of the room as Eoghan talks to her. I know the questions she'll ask off by heart: she always starts with, 'Have you checked your temperature today?' Then, 'Any nausea? Dizziness? Pain or swelling in your legs?' the latter being a sign of a blood clot. We'd called the nurse for advice multiple times over the course of his treatment – usually over-worrying about minor side effects. Between Eoghan and my father, I was now quite confident there was nothing I hadn't seen or couldn't handle. It took a lot now to shock me, and one blurred eye was child's play.

I walk back into the living room as Eoghan replaces the handset on the phone.

'They want me to go in, straight away.'

I thought I knew it all, but the doctors knew far more. Blurred vision was a warning sign: a siren-red, flashing light. They know it's a brain tumour as soon as they take his phone call. By lunchtime that day, the results of a scan confirm there are two: inoperable because of their positioning and size.

They immediately admit Eoghan as an in-patient. He is happier in hospital, under the watchful eye of the doctors, but I badly want to take him home with me: I hate driving away and leaving him there. A new course of radiotherapy will begin the next day, focusing on the two cancerous spots on his brain.

Whilst Eoghan is distracted, absorbed in a game of football being shown on the ward's big-screen TV, his doctor talks me through the treatment. I ask him to predict the outcome, going on the success rate, but he says every patient differs and it's impossible to guess. Big chicken, I think.

When I visit Eoghan the next day he tells me that he has made two friends on the ward called Abdul and Paul.

'Last night I said a prayer for them both,' he says quietly, although I'd never known Eoghan to be religious. 'They're not like me, you know, Ames. They're really sick. They may die soon.'

I nod, smile fixedly and thank God he doesn't know any better. Whether it's through ignorance or avoidance, his denial is a blessing.

That evening, as I'm driving home through a gale, Eoghan, tucked up in his bed on the ward, writes in his diary quite jovially:

3 April 2007. Say hello to my new companion – my little brain melanoma. Welcome to the team.

My parents, sadly, know only too well what it means when I phone home to tell them the cancer has spread to Eoghan's brain. They don't tell me at the time. No, at the time they fix their eyes on the silver lining and only ever speak optimistically to Eoghan and me. But, many months after Eoghan's death, when I am settled in London and less fragile of mind, my mother will show me a page taken from her diary, which was written the same day Eoghan wrote his entry.

3 April 2007. I came home from work today to find Steve washing up cups in the kitchen. I watched him drying them carefully with a tea towel, paying an unnatural amount of attention to the cleaning of their handles. He looked out of the kitchen window and calmly mentioned he had a 'bit of bad news'. Eoghan has lost partial sight in one eye. The melanoma has travelled to Eoghan's brain.

I know it was Steve's heroic attempt to convey the worst news possible in the gentlest way. But I also know this has destroyed any last hope that Eoghan can survive.

So now, God, please hear me. I ask you for a deal.

I'm on my hands and knees as I write this.

Please listen. Please let me swap places with Eoghan.

You see, I don't know if you understand, but you would get a better deal with me dying.

I mean, I've had a brilliant time: married for nearly 30 years to the love of my life. You've given me two beautiful girls, and helped me raise them to be nice people.

I have had my turn and am really OK about being given cancer and everything that goes with it, so give it to me and take it away from my Eoghan, my lovely, lovely man.

I don't care where you put it. Stick it in my neck, my leg, it really doesn't bother me.

If you can make it quick that would be good, but if not, don't worry.

I want to do a trade with you: I want to swap my life for Eoghan's. People would miss me but they would get over it. They would say, 'Well, she had a wonderful life' and 'The girls will look after their dad.'

I can't watch Eoghan die and watch Amy unfold and fall apart. This horror could end if you agree to this. Please, please, I am begging you, do this for me. Let me off the hook.

The dying bit would be easy compared to bearing this.

When I spoke to my mother that evening I remember her saying I had to have faith, that they can treat brain tumours, and that this wasn't the time to give up hope. Eoghan was sitting in the chair next to me when I replied, so I said the only thing I could: 'I know. They'll treat it. Radiotherapy will shrink it.'

Of all the conversations I had with my family back then, did any of us mean what we were saying? Sure, the words we said were definitively optimistic, but none of us was totally convincing – apart from Eoghan, who I do think believed, determinedly, he would survive. With the same determination that my mother prayed that she would die.

9 *April 2007*

Five days after his radiotherapy started, the doctors let Eoghan go home. The remaining fifteen doses could be administered to him as an outpatient. He is ecstatic, and says it's the best news he's had since he was first diagnosed. He dances around the family room of the oncology ward, planting kisses on the cheeks of the nurses, and envelops his doctor in a bear hug. I'm reserved, waiting for the comedown that's sure to follow. His emotions are elevated by a high dose of steroids and his moods veer between euphoria and anger without reason. On the way home he snaps at me that I'm driving too slowly. When I speed up he vomits in the foot-well of the car. Now you see what I'm up against.

Back at home, I tuck Eoghan into bed and stroke his hairless head until he falls asleep. I unpack his overnight bag and find his diary, tucked in the inside pocket, almost full now of drawings and scribbles. Often, Eoghan reads his diary aloud to me, so I don't feel guilty now as I open it and scan his last entry.

8 April. 10 a.m. Feeling good, small headache. Puked this morning and brought up all my breakfast. What a waste. But what great news to come: the best news I've had since diagnosis. I'm going home today. I can be treated as an outpatient. I'm so happy, I can go back home, to my love, my rock, Amy. The sun is splitting the sky. I can't wait to be cuddled up in bed with her.

I'm crying a lot, but only because of the medication. I suppose that's what all these chemicals do to you. I wonder sometimes how long it will be before I'm well again. But it'll all be worth it in the end. I'm fighting for my life, for the woman I love.

I close the diary quietly and replace it in the inside pocket of the duffel bag. I check that Eoghan's still sleeping then step out of the stuffy bedroom, walk down the hallway to the kitchen and then out into the fresh air of the garden, taking a long shuddering breath in. I used to love the twee-ness and cosiness of our studio apartment, but as the weeks pass the walls are closing in and it seems filled with the foggy stench of hospital waiting rooms and cleaning fluid. At least in the garden I'm not hemmed in.

I wonder if Eoghan knows he's losing the fight. Though it pains me to admit it, it's clear the doctors have sent him home to help him enjoy the short time he has left. It can only be a matter of time before they call off chemotherapy completely. His shattered body won't be able to take the strain of it much longer. And then what will I do? How will I keep him going? How will I keep him alive on my own?

To keep myself busy, and stop my mind from over-thinking, I fetch a grass-stained plastic bucket from the shed at the base of the garden, fill it with suds and boiling water, and weave down the garden path to the car. As I scrub at the carpet in the foot-well where he'd vomited, the chemi-cals in his stomach bile stain my fingers yellow. I don't wear gloves. There's something deeply satisfying about the water scalding the skin on my hands, just bordering on unbear-able. Specks of vomit flick into the air and spray my cheeks. Like a mother with her baby, I love him enough not to care. I love every element of him; absurdly, even this. It's that moment I decide that if he doesn't survive I will find a way to die. Yes, that's what I'll do. Eoghan, wherever you go, I'll follow you. Once I've made the choice I'm instantly calm, knowing wherever he goes I won't be far behind.

I hadn't planned to share this decision with Eoghan, but as we lie in bed that night, shoulder to shoulder in the darkness, my fingers looped through his, trying not to press on the puncture wound from his IV drip, the admission spills out involuntarily.

'Eoghan,' I say, already wondering if it's too late to stop myself and realizing it is. 'Just listen to me and don't say anything, OK? Whilst you were in hospital and I was here, alone, I had a lot of time to think; too much time to think probably.

'I know you're going to beat this cancer, I've told you I have faith in that. But if for any reason, *any* reason, you die –' I break off, realizing it sounds like I've given up hope, and backtrack quickly. 'I mean, you might not die from cancer, you might be hit by a car, or run over by a bus, or anything . . .'

He cuts me off: 'Amy, what are you trying to say?'

I take a breath and say it simply: 'I've decided if you ever die I'm going to kill myself to be with you.'

We lie in silence. A shard of moonlight cuts through the curtains and draws a line across the duvet, straight between us. For almost an hour we lie there like strangers until I can take this no longer.

'Eoghan?' I start softly, sitting up in bed and peering through the darkness at the silhouette of his face: 'Are you OK?'

He sits up with a jerk, to challenge me, his eyes tunnelling through mine. His brow is furrowed, his mouth set in a stony line. When he speaks he spits his words like venom: 'How could you?' he snarls. 'Who the fuck are you?'

My eyes widen in horror. I have never seen him show such revulsion. What is happening, what have I done to him?

'You selfish little girl.' His words splinter me like bullets:

'Who the fuck do you think you are to decide? Can't you think about anyone but yourself? You selfish, stupid brat.'

I sit as rigid in bed as a mannequin, shell-shocked and bitterly hurt. I have cared for him, bathed him, cradled him through six months of treatment and still he thinks I'm selfish because I'd dare to give up life for him as well.

And still he vents on: 'If you choose to die you will destroy your parents' lives; you'll kill your sister, your cousins and your grandparents. They'll never forgive themselves. And I tell you now, Amy, I will never ever forgive you. If you want to do that, then fine, go jump off a building, but I won't be waiting for you. I'd never come near you, I'd never be able to look you in the face again.

'I thought I knew you, Amy.' His voice drops, his anger ebbs, he has run out of steam. 'I thought you were stronger than this.'

I string together the only words I have in my memory: 'I'm sorry. I'm scared.'

Eoghan covers his face with his hands, his shoulders heave and he starts to cry. Months of pent-up emotion thunder from his body and the air ripples in waves with the force of his sobs.

'Promise me,' he says chokingly. 'Please promise you'll never do it. You have to promise me you'll keep living even if I have to leave.'

I have nothing left inside of me. An empty shell; I am hollow and empty, exhausted and deathly lonely, even with him beside me. However, I would do anything to make him happy. 'I promise,' I tell him, nodding.

I don't know why I told Eoghan about my suicide plans that evening. I had certainly never intended to. But I never forgot that promise and, in the early days after Eoghan died, it was that conversation which kept me alive.

Chapter Eight

This weekend marks a low point in my grieving process. On both Friday and Saturday night I get incoherently drunk: spill pints, pick fights and generally lose my integrity completely. On Sunday I stoop one stage lower and, in desperate need of a pick-me-up, I call Tyler. I know, I know, I was doing so well. The last text I sent him said, 'Don't come near me again,' and I had lasted a fortnight with no contact and no regrets. But on Sunday morning I wake with my ego in the gutter. I need a hit of him. Nothing else will take the sour taste of the weekend away.

Waking with a throbbing hangover, I send Tyler a text at 8 a.m.: 'I miss you. I want to see you.'

It is the day of the London Marathon and I have already made plans with Rachel to spend a boozy afternoon by the course in Temple, but I hope to persuade Tyler to join us.

An hour later he replies to my plea: 'I'm just jumping in the shower then I'm all yours for the day.'

All mine for the day? This is truly a first: he normally drops round for a fleeting hour between leaving work and going home to *her*.

'I'm watching the race in a bar in Temple,' I reply. 'Come and meet us there.'

This is a risky strategy. As a rule, Tyler doesn't venture out of his North London comfort zone to see me. The odd dates we go on are to local bars, and I know, deep down, that if I lived more than four miles from his house, he'd rarely make it round to see me. Tyler likes convenience: a doting fiancée at home and a girlfriend practically on his doorstep. Asking him to travel South is pushing it.

My phone rings. 'You're having a laugh, aren't you?' His tone is unfriendly: 'I'm not getting on some train. Stay at home and I'll come over.'

'I can't stay at home.' My stomach has tied itself in knots and I know my voice bleats with desperation. These days I hate confrontation: 'I promised Rachel I'd go with her. Please put yourself out, just this once; for me. It's an easy journey. Just come with us.'

Silence and then: 'I'm going to jump in the shower. Then I'll call you back in a minute.' He cuts off the call without a goodbye. He isn't convinced I'm worth the effort.

Bolstered by Rachel, I get dressed, jump on a bus and, an hour later, we are settled in a Walkabout pub with a medicinal Jack Daniels. This is a worrying sign of my state of mind, as I only ever turn to whiskey in times of turmoil, and never before 10 p.m. Today, I order a double at one minute past midday. I am the first in line when the bar opens. By the time I can see the bottom of the glass, he has still not called me back.

One more drink in, I can't hold my tongue any longer

and send a rambling text, the words spilling into two messages, then three: 'I've been looking forward to seeing you. You say you love me; well, actions speak louder than words. If you can't even be arsed to get on a tube to Temple for me then I don't want to see you again. You need me more than I need you. Go home to your fiancée. I hope you die of boredom.'

Why do I think this will persuade him? I regret it the moment the message is sent. No man reacts well to an ultimatum, particularly a man with a fiancée to fall back on.

His reply is short and proves my point. 'You're a spoilt brat, Amy,' it states curtly. That's just perfect.

Fuck him, I think. I've put up with enough. I've moved heaven and earth for him in the past: I was prepared to give him everything he asked, and he won't even travel a few stops on the Underground. Enough is enough.

I am in a black mood.

'He's acting like a tosser.' Rachel tries to pep me up: 'He's on an ego trip, and the best thing you could do now is ignore him. Don't give him the satisfaction of seeing he's upset you. Look around, Ames, we're surrounded by men. Today you'll meet someone much kinder then Tyler, a proper gentleman who knows how to treat a woman.'

I follow her gaze across the crowded bar. A blond sporting a Cambridge rugby shirt makes eye contact and smiles. Not normally my type, but maybe I should go against the grain for once.

I turn back to her and grin: 'You're right, Rach. I'm sorry, I know you're right. I'm back in the game; I'm not going to let Tyler ruin my day.' I clink her drink with my empty glass. 'Another round?'

I am just settling back at the table with a single for me and a secret double for Rachel when I feel a tap on my shoulder. I turn to find the handsome Rugby Shirt standing behind me.

'Can I help you?' I ask girlishly. His hair is styled with the floppy fringe of a public-school boy. Maybe this is the way forward, I think, a man with breeding and manners is more likely to respect old-fashioned romance than a labourer.

The floppy-fringed stranger places his hand on my shoulder and leans in to whisper in my ear. 'Have you ever before met a man,' he says, 'who finds it impossible to ejaculate from a girl giving him head?'

My expression freezes. I am speechless. This day just gets more and more depressing.

I turn my back on him without responding and sit back down, hoping he'll take the hint and walk away. Thankfully, after a moment, he does.

'What? What did he say?' Rachel asks, but before I have a chance to explain her face falls, she grabs my arm and nods rigidly over my shoulder, eyes bulging.

'Shit,' she mutters. 'Amy; it's Tyler.'

I can't believe it. I wish I could say it is too little too late; that I sneer at his efforts and send him on his way, but I can't. Instead I fly into his arms.

'You're here,' I cheer animatedly, looping my arms around his neck, clutching on to him. He picks me off my feet, folding his arms tightly around me, whilst nodding to plant a kiss on my shoulder. I shake with the relief that he came through for me. This man has turned my day on its head and I can't wipe the grin off my face. I remember this feeling from when I first dated Eoghan. Maybe I am in love after all.

We stay in the pub for the rest of the day. My euphoria rises when I hear Hannah is away at her parents' for the weekend. He tells me he's sleeping over. For the first night in months I won't have to wake alone.

But the next morning, at 7 a.m., I wake up without him. He has left me a note, propped on my bedside cabinet: 'I thought I'd better go home,' it says. I register that it isn't signed off with a kiss.

I lie motionless on my stomach, cheek resting on my pillow, staring at the piece of paper, which he'd ripped out from my journal. I cast my mind back. We'd arranged to go for breakfast together this morning – a long leisurely brunch before Hannah came back from her parents'. What could I have done to make him leave so suddenly? I need to speak to him and find out what happened.

As I turn over from my stomach to reach for my house phone, I yelp in alarm as a pain shoots down my left-hand side. I sit up in bed and crane my neck. My shoulder is covered in deep, jagged bite marks. Fresh purple bruises lead down my arm to a patch of red-raw skin at my elbow. I leap out of bed and stand naked in front of the mirror. Raised scratch marks criss-cross my stomach and what appears to be five fingerprints bruise my left breast. I roll my shoulders gingerly and wince. I feel like I've been in a boxing ring. What the hell happened last night? And how could I have let it?

I pull on my most comforting tracksuit bottoms, but it's hard to find a top that doesn't irritate the broken skin on my shoulder blades. In the end I throw on a vest that is comfortably baggy from over-washing. Because, really, how can I complain? Ask anyone who knows me, they'll tell you I'm no prude. As long as it's not anal, I don't generally say no. This doesn't count as abuse. So why do I feel so used?

This has to be my wake-up call. This dirty, masochistic sex is what married men use call girls for. He doesn't love me, he loves her. I'm just his personal Belle de Jour. Tyler confessed to me before that he has a collection of eighty-five porno films. I'm just one of many pussies in his X-rated fantasies.

I send him a message: 'I can't do this any more.'

So, what to do about my lack of self-will? I know it is all a reaction to the bereavement, but I refuse to consider therapy. I've always said that, unless you'd met Eoghan and knew him personally, it was impossible to grasp the straw roots of our relationship.

Antidepressants are a definite no-no: my mother's been pumped full of Prozac for years, since her own father died when I was a teenager, and is so totally reliant on the drug she's terrified to drop her dose, even though the doctors tell her she should after all this time. Yes, she appears strong on the outside, and is a driving force in my life, but I'd rather know I can cope with life on my own, not because I'm highly medicated. No: I am the only one who can change this.

I need to set some ground rules, to rein myself in before

my reputation is unsalvageable. One-night affairs are no longer enough and, though I shudder to admit it, I want a relationship. Unfortunately, since Eoghan, my seduction technique has changed dramatically: a couple of tequila shots and I'll lock lips with anybody. This sort of behaviour is unlikely to lead to a long-term relationship. It does, however, explain why I'm a magnet for cheats, chauvinists and men with questionable fetishes.

The question is, am I mentally unbalanced from bereavement or just another single woman with a run-of-the-mill yearning? I know many a girl obsessed with the search for Mr Right, but when does loneliness become lunacy? I know the first thing I have to do is cut out alcohol. From this point on I will be teetotal. I need to regain control. The second thing to do is up my search for a job. The isolation of working from home is doing me no good. Lastly, I need to start dating: actual dates with dinner and talking. Real interaction with men whose surnames it's worth learning.

I grab a thick black marker pen and make another sign: 'No booze. Enough bad choices.'

I stick it to my mirror, smack bang in the centre, where even my averted eyes can't ignore it. I feel better already. It's a step in the right direction, at least.

I accept an invitation to dinner from a twenty-five-year-old student called Jonathon – a Canadian who's recently moved to London. I met him in a bar two or three weeks back, where he'd kissed me quite sweetly, asked for my number and the next day called to invite me to dinner. I'd said I was busy – out of some illogical loyalty to Tyler. Now I think, what harm can one date do?

I meet Jonathon at his rented flat in Paddington. He said it would be easier to meet him there, where we could have a quick drink, then walk to this nice Indian restaurant he knows. I agree this sounds fine, and arrive on his doorstep, fifteen minutes early at 7.45.

I'm dressed quite conservatively, in a black knee-length dress made of feather-light silk with spaghetti straps that have a habit of slipping off my shoulders. Just before I leave my house I feel underdressed and grab a green cashmere cardigan to cover my modesty. I remind myself this is a grown-up date and not just a race to fourth base.

Sadly, Jonathon doesn't agree with this sentiment. He buzzes me up to his third-floor flat and kisses me as soon as I step past the front door. I'm quite happy with this – rather that than wait all night for the first kiss. But when he doesn't break away and his hands snake up from my waist, I twist away and joke: 'Aren't you going to offer me a drink?'

He looks put out for a second, then recovers himself and says: 'A vodka and soda? Make yourself at home.' He points at the larger of the two sofas in the room, and I sit to the left-hand side, tucking my dress underneath my knees.

He walks back into the living room carrying two large tumblers of vodka, and places them both on the coffee table, just out of my reach.

'Come and give me a kiss,' he says.

OK, I think, this is familiar enough territory for me, and I lean over to kiss him. But something doesn't feel right. His kisses are too rough, his hands are too free – and what about having a conversation first?

As he tries to push me back on to the sofa, I push him off and attempt small talk.

'So, what did you do today?' I ask.

'Not much,' is all he manages before his mouth is pushed back on to mine, his tongue between my lips and down my windpipe. Why am I feeling panicked? I'm no saint, no fucking virgin. This is what I do: sex is where I normally excel. I force myself to relax and kiss him back. As kisses go, it's not bad, it's quite nice. But as he pushes my dress up my thigh and fumbles for the edge of my knickers, my stomach twists into knots.

This isn't what I signed up for. I signed up for a date, for fuck's sake, I came here for dinner. I don't mind a one-night stand when your cards are laid on the table, but don't tie it up in a yellow ribbon, with false pretence and promises. Give me some credit to make my own choices. Give me some credit to be worth a lot more.

'Get off, Jonathon,' I snap, as he starts to knead my clit, through my knickers, with his fingertips. 'I didn't come here to fuck you.'

'Relax, Amy,' he says, unfastening his belt. 'What's your problem? We're just having fun. I thought you'd be up for anything.'

This knocks me for six. He thinks I'm that sort of girl. Less than a year on from becoming a widow I'm now branded with 'whore'. Is that the message I give off now? Can he smell sex on me? Maybe I should give in: just sleep with him. It would be bearable. He seems competent enough. He'll know what to do, and what goes where at least. Then I can leave straight after and at least he won't think I'm a tease.

I consider this. It's terrifying that I almost choose this

option. Then I look at his face, red and clammy with sweat, and I know I don't want to be that girl any longer.

'I'm leaving,' I say, standing up from the sofa and re-arranging my dress. He looks quite amazed, and I wait for him to back down, to apologize, to try and resuscitate the date. But he doesn't. Instead, as I bend to tie the laces on my shoes, he stands before me, drops his trousers, and rubs his erect penis in my face.

I leap back, and my hand shoots to my mouth.

He stands in the living room, trousers around his ankles, and his penis now wilting and held in his hand. His parting words are: 'Won't you just suck it before you go?'

I have no response. I just want out. I grab my handbag and coat from an armchair and make for the front door. As I yank the door open and step into the stairwell I turn and spit at him: 'You're fucking unbelievable. You don't want a date, you want a hooker.'

'Stop overreacting, Amy,' he says, and slams the door in my face.

On the walk back to the station, my anger ebbs and I start to feel a bit sorry for myself.

So much for dating and turning over a new leaf. Even with the best of intentions, I still end up half naked, being groped by a madman. My phone rings, and I naively think it might be him, calling to apologize for his behaviour, but when I check the display it's my mother.

'Hello, Mama,' I say. 'I've just had the worst date ever.'

And because my mum and I, after all we've been though, have an unusually close relationship, I am able to tell her, without censoring anything, exactly what just happened in Jonathon's living room.

Her response surprises me.

'Amy, I'm so proud of you,' she says. 'Six months ago, you'd have slept with that man. You were so fragile back then. You'd never have had the strength to walk away. Now look how far you've come.'

I look at myself and I do see it. I see the baby step I've taken forward. And the barrier behind me that means I can't, and won't, go back.

The next day I make more changes. I realize I'm bored. That I have too much white space in my days – too much free time which Tyler once filled. I need purpose. I need a real job. So I send emails to every media contact I can think of, along with a copy of the article I wrote about Eoghan for the *Mail on Sunday*. It makes my skin crawl even to look at the headline, but I know that's just a personal grievance. The subject matter is tough, but I know the writing is good, and if anything makes an employer sit up and take notice, this will. I cross my fingers, and hope they don't feel sorry for me. I want to get a job on my writing skills alone, not on the sympathy vote.

The following Thursday, three days later, I'm interviewed for an internship with the *Daily Mail*. I get it, on a two-week basis, but at the end of the fortnight they apparently like me and ask me to stay on as a researcher. It's a wonderful novelty to call my parents with some good news. And to feel I've done something worthwhile of my own accord.

Until the moment when one of my colleagues asks if my surname is Irish, and I say: 'Yes, my dad's family is from Dublin.' It's a stupid, autopilot lie, and I don't know why I say it, because as soon as the words hit my tongue they burn through the flesh and I feel like I've betrayed my husband.

When Eoghan first died, I talked about him 24/7. I'd namedrop him constantly in every conversation. I'd tell shopkeepers, bus drivers, anyone that would listen. I needed everyone to realize that I wasn't just a normal girl because: 'My husband's just died.'

I needed to explain: to justify why I walked around with a face ugly and distorted with pain.

When I moved into the house share in Islington, I stopped talking about Eoghan out loud. His name would pop up in passing, but I didn't monologue about my dead husband as I used to when I lived at my parents'. That was a new beginning, a new chapter in my life, and it didn't feel fair to discuss Eoghan with my housemates, when they didn't even know him. I thought it would bore them.

I certainly didn't want to discuss my dead husband with the men I met and took home. But in my head I'd still constantly talk to him: kiss his cheek goodnight and hold his hand until I fell asleep, even when I had other company in bed with me.

Then that changed as well, although it was a sub-conscious shift at first. I stopped greeting Eoghan in the morning and saying I loved him at night. I stopped refer-encing him in conversations and counting the months since he died. And once I shook the habit, life got easier without him in it. So I banned myself from talking to him completely. I held my tongue when his name sat on its tip. For my own sake, and to survive this, I white-washed over him.

I hold my left hand in front of me. You would never guess now that I'd once worn a wedding ring. I've done a good job hiding my marital status and erasing all evidence of Eoghan's existence. Too good a job, some might say. I try to picture his face, but see a blend of male features blurring together, and I don't think any of them are his. OK, think of the way he used to stroke your hair. I draw a blank. Nothing. Fuck. No! I can't remember him. Think, Amy, think, think. Your wedding day – when he kissed you at the altar – remember. But I can't. My mind's blank: just a mess of blurred images which mean nothing to me.

I run to the bathroom, rock my body over the sink and retch. Oh my God, he's gone, I've pushed him away. Saliva fills my mouth and I gag but can't bring anything up. The badness is a part of me. My body is disgusted at itself.

I stare into the plughole, stunned, watching the debris swirl down the drain. I buried his memory, but I dug down too deep, and now it seems there's no way to unearth him.

It's my fault. I chose to, the moment I told Tyler I loved him. I knew Eoghan would never approve and I couldn't give him the chance to criticize. So I compartmentalized them both: kept Tyler in my world and sent Eoghan to another. It seemed the only thing to do.

I slide on to the cool floor of the bathroom and press my clammy forehead against the shower screen. Was that me who ripped up a letter from Ireland without opening the envelope? Was that me who deleted a computer file full of our photographs because I couldn't stand to have his face in my laptop? Was that me who, just yesterday, threw a whole shoebox of his love letters away?

I miss my husband. I do. This is hard to admit. I miss him so much I've rubbished every part of him left.

26 July 2007

I can pinpoint the first day I began to box Eoghan away: the first brick I put in the wall between me, him and yesterday's pain. It was three weeks after Eoghan died, my parents were back in the UK and I was barely functioning, semi-existing in a state of daydream. But still I had formalities to attend to. So I got the tram into Dublin city and marched resolutely into the county registry office. The gentleman who manned the reception desk was greying and wrinkled. He smiled kindly as I approached. I didn't smile back; my mouth was set. I was determined to be emotionless, to complete my task and get out fast. 'I need to register my marriage,' I began. The old man smiled approvingly. 'And my husband's death,' I finished. His smile vanished.

I took my place in the sterile waiting area, looked around and thought: now whose bright idea was it to register deaths in the same office you go to in order to register births? It was an obvious and unsympathetic error in planning. The waiting room was full that day – full of couples cradling their newborn babies, staring into each other's eyes, full of the joys of a new life. I was the only person in the room alone and obviously the only person registering a death. I was twenty-three years old; this was very wrong. I stood out like a sore thumb.

I waited fifty minutes before my name was called by the

registrar. In that time I watched six couples come and go. They didn't glance at me – why should they? They were in their own wonderful worlds, blinkered by their bonny babies. I didn't have the strength to hate them. I was too weary to muster an emotion that strong. Instead I sat and stared at a patch of damp on the wall, the plastic seat of the chair glued to my thighs with sweat. I clutched my handbag like a buoyancy aid – it held my wedding certificate and a formal letter from the hospital confirming Eoghan's time of death. In a locket round my neck hung a photograph of Eoghan, taken on our wedding day, and a lock of his hair I saved from when we shaved him bald for chemo. It was all I had left.

When my turn came the registrar called my name four times before she noticed me. Who can blame her? She had been handed a form with nothing but my name and details: Amy Molloy, registering death of husband, Eoghan Molloy. She was looking for a widow, and the young girl, practically a child, sitting in a sundress in the corner wasn't it. Even when I raised my hand she still looked through me. Finally, I gathered my energy, rose to my feet and approached her. 'That's me,' I said, and she did a relatively good job of hiding her surprise.

The registrar's name badge introduced her as Helen. After seating me in a green melamine chair, Helen typed my name into the system and uploaded my details on to her computer screen. She checked my paperwork then registered my marriage first. Miss Amy Maria Collins: married to Mr Eoghan Patrick Joseph Molloy, 4 June 2007.

A phone rang in a neighbouring office and, swearing lightly, Helen excused herself to answer it. I counted seven minutes before she returned. I don't know why, but time seemed suddenly important. I sat and whispered seconds like a schoolchild: one Mississippi, two Mississippi, three Mississippi. After 420 Mississippis Helen came back into the room, apologizing for the delay. She swiftly logged the date of Eoghan's death on to her computer and pressed enter. An hourglass spun on the screen as it updated my status. I blinked. When I looked again my status had changed: Ms Amy Maria Molloy: widow. For seven minutes I was a wife. For seven minutes I officially had a husband. Tears prickled the corners of my eyes.

'Is that all for today?' Helen asked.

'Yes, yes,' I replied, nodding. 'I think that's enough.'

On the tram home to Dalkey I took off my wedding ring. I placed it in my palm and looked at it questioningly. Then I put it back on. I took it off. I put it back on. I took it off again. Finally, I left it on. I wore my wedding ring until 2 January 2008, six months after Eoghan died, and then I took it off for good. I gave it to my mum to look after. She keeps it by her bed in a crystal keepsake box, along with a pressed flower from my wedding bouquet. I doubt I'll ever wear it again. I tried it on the last time I visited my parents. It doesn't fit me any more, though I don't mean in the physical sense. It doesn't fit who I've become.

The same applies to my wedding dress. I've tried it on only once since my wedding day, the day I left Ireland and came home to England. I was in the process of packing the last of my belongings and the metre square box was laid out on my desktop, waiting to be placed in the removal van.

Since the wedding, I'd kept the dress under my bed, but now the bed's frame was flat-packed, I could no longer avoid it. It had been professionally cleaned and, before it was boxed, they had wrapped it in candied swirls of tissue paper, sprinkled with confetti in the shape of Cupid and arrowed hearts. I lace my fingers under the lid of the box and with a shuffle lift it clean off its base in one, just as they tell you to rip off a Band-Aid. I peel back the corners of the tissue paper, too scared to touch the fabric of the dress itself. My fingertip catches velvet and, as I pull the paper back, with it comes a green ribbon, with an edge forked like the tongue of a snake. It winds around my wrist and only tightens as I try to shake it off. It pulls my hand down into the folds of fabric and whispers: Just try it on, one more time.

I pull my hooded jumper over my head and shake my tracksuit bottoms to my ankles. I undress completely, hands shaking so much I can't undo the clasp of my bra, so I drag it over my shoulders and head in one piece, before stepping out of my knickers. I reach for the dress and clasp the bony lip of the bodice in both hands, unfolding it from the box like a concertina, length after length of train that's never-ending. My skin, quite remarkably, is paler than the dress, which is only one shade off snow-white itself.

I'd had the dress drycleaned after the wedding simply because I had a free voucher for a bespoke dry cleaner's, but now I wish I'd left the grass stains on its hem. Spotlessly clean, with no sign of wear, it looks like the dress of a jilted lover who was left at the altar but harbours the dress in the back of her closet. From this dress there's no evidence a wedding took place.

My knuckles are even whiter still, as I reach for the zipper, undo it to the waist and pull the dress over my head. It takes me a moment to find a route through the skirts: each way I twist there's a dead end or a double-stitched hem. I scramble through fabric that gets thicker and fuller as my heartbeat grows faster, battling through cloth to find the neckline. The fingers on my right hand touch air and, with relief, I find I'm through. But something doesn't feel right. As I unfold the dress over my silhouette, it bunches and refuses to cooperate. The fabric pulls and scratches at my skin. Though I've lost and gained no weight since my wedding day, the dress which used to mould my skin now hangs from my bust and pinches at my waist uncomfortably. I reach to pull up the zip, but it catches halfway and nips at the skin above my spine, drawing blood. We used to fit like a glove, this dress and I; three months ago we were a perfect partnership. Everyone said so.

25 *May 2007*

I remember the morning I bought it, ten days before our wedding and fourteen days after we were told Eoghan had two months to live.

I should have been excited, on the way to have my wedding dress fitted. It was every little girl's dream – and not only that, but it was at Vera Wang. Under normal circumstances, I would have been uncontrollable. But there was nothing normal about this.

I had left Eoghan in the care of his best man, with a

list of instructions and emergency contact numbers. He was in good hands, but still I was nervous, checking my phone at one-minute intervals in case I missed a call. Eoghan had thrown himself into organizing the wedding and, although I understood it took his mind off other things, I could also see it was draining him. It'd be an ending fit for Hollywood, I thought, if he dies as I'm trying on my wedding gown. I didn't want to leave him. I certainly didn't want to go shopping.

As I walked through the arched doorway of Vera Wang I spotted the wives of two of Eoghan's groomsmen waiting for me. They'd offered to come, knowing my bridesmaids were back in England, and though I was thankful to have them there for moral support, all I wanted was my mum. I'd got an email from her that morning.

My darling Amy

    I wanted to call to wish you luck but I thought it best to email in case I get tearful. You know what I'm like – I get so over-emotional, and that's the last thing you need today of all days.

    Because today, my baby girl, you're off to buy your wedding dress. And although you act tough and feign independence, I bet today you'd like your mother with you, wouldn't you? I feel I've abandoned you. I've deserted you on the one day a mother should be there. And for that, I'm so sorry.

    Over the years I have, like any mother, dreamed of going out shopping with my beloved girls for their wedding gowns: more so you than your sister because she's always been more of a tomboy. I've

imagined us, sipping champagne, debating on
styles, laughing at meringue monstrosities: traipsing
around every shop, trying on, crying, laughing and
then after all that going back to the first one that
you had liked but that I had put you off! I can
imagine it exactly.

It breaks my heart that I'm not with you today. I
remember when you were four months old,
dressing you in your christening dress. You gurgled
and dribbled all over it, kicking your legs and
wriggling all the way to the church. But as soon as
we got you on the altar, in front of an audience,
you sat up straight and flashed a model smile. You
were like a beautiful little angel.

And remember your First Holy Communion
dress? I bought it in Laura Ashley and you loved it
so much you wore it for two days afterwards. In
your hair sat my bridal circlet of flowers – the
same one I wore when marrying your daddy. Isn't
that wonderful? I bought that in Selfridges on my
way home from work one night, two months
before my wedding day. The flowers had curled in
on themselves by the time it came to your
communion, but my own mother, God rest her
soul, stood over a boiling kettle and steamed the
petals open one by one.

I always presumed that I would be woven into
the fabric of your wedding gown too. Then again,
I thought a lot of things would be different.

I spent hours at work yesterday trawling
through the Vera Wang website trying to guess

which dress you might pick: knowing it will be the most original and non-frilly bridal gown in existence, because I trust that you have exquisite taste and a strong idea of who you are. There's one dress I think would be perfect for you, although I won't tell you which, not yet anyway, because I don't want to sway your opinion. But I did print off a picture and as I write this it's propped up next to my keyboard. It has a touch of green to it, but that's all I will tell you (and don't roll your eyes, Ame, it is lovely).

Do you remember the wedding dress you cut out of a fashion magazine, when you were about fifteen? The one with the wired skirt in the shape of a fairground carousel, with red and white swirls and carousel horses printed on it? You kept that page pressed in your diary for years and always said it was the dress that you wanted to get married in. You had your mind set on it, no matter how much we laughed at you. It was so typically Amy: always eccentric.

I know whichever dress you choose will be perfect. Trust me, my little one: you'll know when you've found the one. It's the dress which makes you want to dance around the room. Even though your feet are leaden with dread.

Don't let the circumstances take away from your special day, my darling. Remember: I may not be there in person but I'm in your heart. I love you, always, and am so proud of you.

Mummy. x

Before I went shopping I printed the email and folded it into the pocket of my jeans. The sharp corners of paper jab my leg through the pocket's lining as I walk. It's oddly comforting.

An assistant rushes up to me: 'You must be Amy. It's so lovely to meet you,' she gushes. 'I'm Germaine, and I'll be helping you today. Step this way and I'll show you our selection. And why don't we all have a glass of champagne?'

As the last syllable of the sentence slips from her lips her eyes widen with horror. She clasps her hands to her mouth, trying to stuff the words back in before I hear.

'Or maybe you'd just like a cup of tea,' she backtracks, and I realize she must have been told of my circumstances. 'Or a glass of water perhaps.'

I want to tell her not to worry. I know she knows so there's no need to pretend. But instead I mutter, 'I really don't mind,' and let my hair fall over my face to hide my flushed cheeks.

I am awkward, shy, and don't feel fit to be here. Rails of swanlike bridal gowns line the walls of the shop, so delicate they seem to hover above their hangers. I catch a glimpse of myself in the baroque framed mirror and grimace, but these days I have no time to take pride in my appearance. My priorities are different.

However, now I wish I'd made a touch more effort. I'm dressed in jeans that have grown baggy from being washed so frequently and a high-street vest top that I only now see has specks of vomit on the bust from when Eoghan projectiled his breakfast that morning. What would Vera say?

'Do you have any idea what style of dress you'd like?' Germaine asks. 'Do you know if you'd prefer it in white, taupe or ivory, silk or organza, with straps or a bodice? Are you considering a train or veil, high heels or flats, with your hair up or down?'

I feel under attack. I don't know the answers: I haven't thought about it. Why hadn't I thought about it? What sort of bride am I?

'Umm, white, I think.' I flounder. 'No veil. And flat shoes.' In my head I'm calculating the most functional options. A veil's not practical, as in all likelihood Eoghan will struggle to manoeuvre around it – his painkillers make him all fingers and thumbs. Knowing Eoghan, and his determination, he'll pull himself together on the day, and be the life and soul of the party no matter how much pain he's in. Still, I'm a realist and certain things need to be thought of. The Amy of Old would have loved five-inch stilettos, the Amy of New needs a firmer footing to support her husband if he loses his balance. I wonder how many other brides choose their outfits based on these criteria?

'OK then.' Germaine moves towards the nearest rail: 'Why don't we try a few different styles and narrow down our options?'

Tall, ornate dresses stand like ladies in waiting, with names like Allegra and Hermione. Auspicious and privileged, chest puffed out in the certain knowledge their special day will be just perfect. I don't fit here, I think. I'm not like them.

As if to prove this further, a second assistant appears from a side room, bearing a tray with three cups of tea and a plate of rustic-looking biscuits. More fitting for a bride in my position, I suppose, but I'd much prefer champagne. This should be my special day.

Germaine pulls four dresses from the rack and leads me into a fitting room elaborately decorated with a royal-purple chaise longue and a velvet curtain so thick I need my full force to draw it to a close. I undress, wearily. My muscles ache and my joints creak and yawn as I bend to untie my trainers. I've been feeling slowly worse each day, since we started planning this wedding. My symptoms resemble flu, but I know I'm not ill. It's like my body can't cope with the sadness any more. I stand in front of the mirror in mismatched knickers and bra and feel utterly inferior to any other bride that's been in here.

I look at the dress on top of the pile. Its ivory bodice has corset hem stitching and a tail that flares out like a mermaid's. It's beautiful, yes, but so wrong for me. It's too ostentatious and almost too beautiful. I'd be lost in its loveliness. I need something simpler.

'I don't want to look too old,' I say quietly. 'And I don't want to look showy. You've probably been told my husband has cancer,' I say, hating that I have to explain. 'They told us he only has two months left. That's why we're getting married.'

I hear myself, and realize what I've just said.

'No, wait.' I clutch Germaine's hands. 'Of course, I'm marrying him because I love him as well. That sounds awful. He'd be devastated to hear me say that.' Oh fuck, fuck, fuck, I can't cry over a £15,000 Vera Wang dress.

Diplomatically, Germaine looks away as I dry my eyes and wipe my running nose on the edge of my sleeve.

'What I mean,' I continue, in a calmer vein, 'is my dress

can't be too showy. But it can't be too dowdy, because I can't look like I'm mourning him. And I need to look pretty – because what if this is the last memory he has of me? On top of that, I want to feel young – I'm only twenty-three, you know – to still feel like me and be comfortable, because it's going to be hard enough getting through this without being trussed up like a flaming turkey.'

I'm fully aware my requirements are unusual, and I'm fully prepared for Germaine to say: there's nothing for you here, you'll have to go elsewhere. But instead she takes my hand and says: 'Trust me, darling. Why don't you try this one on for size?' and pulls a dress, soon to be My Dress, from the back of the pile.

It's perfect, and I know I'll buy this dress, before I either try it on or check the price tag. It's strapless, with an empire waist rimmed by a green velvet sash. The bodice is cut from coffee-coloured organza and the skirt, swathes of ivory which lead into a train that swims around my heels.

'A Midsummer Night's Dream,' I mutter under my breath.

'Yes, it is rather Shakespearean,' says Germaine.

'More than that, it's the dress I imagine Hermia would have.' I allow the dress to be slipped over my head. 'And even she got her happy ever after in the end.'

Forty minutes later, with the dress pinned and ready to be altered, Germaine emerges from behind the reception desk with a bottle of Cristal champagne.

'Now you, my fairy-tale bride, have something to celebrate,' she says. In the end, I even choose a veil.

Chapter Nine

It's time to move forward. And to move forward I need to look back. It is time to revisit what I loved about Eoghan, the lessons he taught me and the good times we had. I can't block him out for ever. That, surely, can't be healthy. And there are a lot of good memories – perfect memories – in my head somewhere.

'OK, Eoghan,' I tell him, 'I'm ready to remember. But you'll need to help me.'

Forty minutes later, right on cue, I find a letter. It's a slothful, quiet Sunday and I'm obscenely bored so decide to tidy my underwear drawer. I find a solitary piece of paper, bunched in the drawstring bag which houses my unnecessary bikinis. I unfold it carefully, unfurling the corners, conscious that it's already been torn. The paper, pulled from a jotting notebook, is covered with my swirling handwriting and has a title written in capitals with heart shapes dotting the 'I's: 'Reasons why I love you. 21 March 2006.'

I do remember writing this. My first love letter to Eoghan: written when we were parked up in our camper van in Noosa. As the title suggests, it's a list of why I love him: it originally ran to two pages, before I edited it down to my top ten. I lay the note flat on top of my chest of drawers and start at the top:

Reasons why I love you. 21 March 2006.

1. For the way you wake me up by whistling to the Boo Radleys' 'Wake Up Boo!' – even when it's pouring.
2. Because you steal me liquorice laces from the newsagent's and plait them into bracelets.
3. For the fact you're more chuffed when I catch a wave than I am.
4. For the way you never judge others, but couldn't care less if they're judging you harshly.
5. Because I've never laughed like this before. Period.
6. Because you have no idea how beautiful you are, or that I pinch myself for finding you.
7. For the way you let me paint your toenails, even in my pinkest varnish. And let me take photographic evidence, to send home to my parents.
8. You make up for every dark day in the past by filling my life with light and love.
9. Because just when I think I can't love you any more, you sing a song or pull a face or trip over your own feet and I fall for you twice as hard.
10. I don't love you in spite of your flaws. I love you because of them.

I come to the end of the page and let the piece of paper slide from my fingertips, on to the floor. I stand in my bedroom. I still don't feel anything.

I step on to the paper, with the bare sole of my foot, hoping I might be sucked into it like Bert through the street art in *Mary Poppins*. If this was a film it would swallow me up and spit me out back in Australia: three years before this, when life was so simple and the mole on Eoghan's chest was nothing but a beauty spot.

In the last few weeks I've been trying to think about Eoghan more, I really have. I've been trying, one day at a time, to pull bricks out of the wall I erected between me and him, letting hazy rays of memory through. Now I've got three whole photographs of him Blu-tacked on my bedroom wall, which is a big step, as they were locked in a box under my bed before. I have to admit I don't look at them, and stubbornly avert my gaze when I walk past them: 'Eyes right' at the photos, like a backwards military salute. I've developed a blind spot to that part of the wall, so really there's no point in the photos being up at all.

Every now and again I stop and force myself to stare at them, but the smiling faces laminated in the photographs mean nothing to me and leave me emotionless. There's one photo of Eoghan, taken the week after the doctors broke the news that the cancer had spread to his brain. You'd never guess by the smile he wears; to look at the photo you'd think he was a young, healthy man with not a care in the world.

13 April 2007

We'd gone away for the weekend, on a trip arranged by the nurse and the hospital and paid for by a local charity.

They sent us to Easkey in County Sligo to watch the Irish National Surf Championships. I couldn't persuade Eoghan to leave his surfboard at home, or to wear a wetsuit to protect his body from the icy Irish Sea: his stubbornness made him impossible to argue with. So, on the Sunday morning, at 7 a.m., we grabbed our boards, found a deserted stretch of beach behind the rocky headland and raced each other into the waves.

I thank God that I had thought to bring my underwater camera, because Eoghan's excitement was spellbinding. By this point he was riddled with cancer from head to toe – his liver, lungs, pancreas, spleen and brain were swollen with the disease – but still I watched as he catapulted himself into the sea, fearless and unperturbed by the rumbling white wash around him. I abandoned my board and instead sat in the shallows, watching. It was moments like this that reminded me what I was fighting for.

I took that photograph as Eoghan re-emerged from the sea. He's laughing wildly at the camera; his cheeks flushed from the cold and crystals of salt glistening on his eyelashes. Unusually for Ireland, the sky is kingfisher-blue and cloudless, and the early morning sun washes across Eoghan's face as he looks up at the heavens and punches the air: 'Yes,' he bellows. 'Take that, cancer. Take that, you fucker! You can't beat me; I'm telling you now, you'll never get us down.'

I drop the camera on to the sand as he sweeps me into his arms and presses his nose against mine. He kisses me softly, the salt from his lips scratching mine; the taste instantly reminds me of Australian sunsets and our backpacking days.

'I'm never going to leave you, Amox,' he promises me. 'I'm going to beat this fucker, you have to trust me on that. We're going to go on and have a family, and one day I'll bring our baby here, to show him this sea and teach him the rhythm of the waves.'

He smiles and cups my cheek in his hand: 'We've got so much to look forward to, Amy; this is just the start, and I know it's been rocky, but it will get easier. Once we get through this, we've got all the time in the world together. I've got big plans for us, bubba.'

Today, looking back at that photograph, I wish I could still be that blissfully naive.

In an effort to reconnect with Eoghan, I sit down to watch the DVD of my wedding for the first time. I'm nervous; indeed my hands shake as I slip the disc into the drawer of the player. The first image flashed on the television is a profile shot of him, dressed in his white morning suit and bowler hat, his eyepatch firmly in place. One of his five groomsmen, Gary, is in charge of the camera and, as we watch, the lens scans the hotel room, where the boys are in various stages of undress.

Eoghan hops up and down on one leg, tying his shoelace whilst glugging from a glass of champagne. Cheeky git, I think: he was on a cocktail of medicines and had promised me he wouldn't touch booze but, oh well, it's not as if I can scold him now!

With both shoes tied, Eoghan straightens his shirt collar, grins at the camera and asks: 'How do I look, boys? Good enough for my beautiful bride?'

I want to leap into the television and grab him, touch

him, smell him, to dig my nails into his skin. I desperately need something tangible to cling to, because I know that when the films reaches its end and I press 'stop', Eoghan will be gone again.

The film cuts to the church, where Eoghan and I stand hand in hand, repeating our vows. As the priest pronounces us husband and wife, Eoghan picks me up and swings me round, and I marvel at how uninhibited I am: my head's thrown back laughing, my sandalled feet are a foot off the ground. The congregation, filled with our family and friends, rise to their feet and almost raise the roof off the church with the volume of their cheer. It's like watching two characters in a Hollywood film. I just can't comprehend that that's me.

The film cuts again, to our reception this time, held in the Brooklodge hotel, a peaceful sanctuary nestled in Wicklow countryside. Eoghan is stood before our guests, coming to the end of his wedding speech. I remember he was surprisingly nervous, which I didn't understand, as he was a naturally confident guy, but now, looking back, I wonder if he saw this as his chance to say goodbye.

He stands at the head of the top table, with a microphone balanced in one hand, a wine glass of orange juice in the other and his eyes locked on the glowing face of his new bride.

'My beautiful girl,' he says, loud enough for the crowd but never taking his eyes from my face: 'I wish I was better with words, so I could explain the deep love I feel for you. From the second I walked into that bar and saw you, with your ridiculous blonde ringlets and the shortest shorts I've ever seen, I was totally knocked out and knew that one day I would marry you. I know this journey we're on sometimes feels like we're walking on thorns, whilst other people's roads are paved with roses, but Amy, no one had ever captured my heart the way you did. We were linked up by the stars with the blessings of the angels.'

His voice breaks and I watch a single tear roll down his cheek before he continues: 'Do you know how invincible I am with you in my corner?' His pitch grows louder, determined now and stronger. 'With you, my angel, I can't be beaten. I am a winner.' Seemingly exhausted, he almost whispers his last sentence: 'I love you, Amy, beyond and for ever.'

The DVD whirs to a stop, the television screen goes blank and Eoghan is snatched away.

I get up to switch off the DVD player and find Rachel behind me, crying quietly into a tissue, her normally perfect make-up running down her cheeks in rivulets.

'I'm sorry, Ame,' she says through her tears. 'I wasn't prying. I came downstairs and saw you were watching it and didn't want to disturb you. But what a wonderful wedding – it all looked so beautiful. What a perfect day.'

I smile, give Rachel a hug and go upstairs. Everyone said that: the guests, the hotel workers, Eoghan – all agreed it was perfect. And it really was. But by the end of the night, it did grate on me somewhat.

Mine and Eoghan's parting words to each other on our wedding night were:

Me: 'Fuck you.'

Him: 'Fuck you too.'

I then slept in the bedroom of the honeymoon suite,

whilst Eoghan slept on the sofa in the living room. By this point we hadn't had sex for six months. This is partly what the barrage of 'fuck you's was all about. Don't get me wrong, I never loved him more than on that day, but we were a young couple, getting married, in the shadow of terminal cancer. This was not your average wedding day. And anyone who says it was perfect is kidding themselves.

Eoghan and I stopped having sex around January – about six months after his initial diagnosis. The chemo was just too strong, the painkillers too numbing, and things, down there, just couldn't work as they should any more. Don't get me wrong, we gave it our best shot, even confiding in our oncology doctors, who said it was perfectly normal and prescribed Eoghan Viagra. But this didn't work either. So the doctors said it was psychological. They hinted that maybe I was putting too much pressure on Eoghan to perform: so much for not placing the blame.

In the end we stopped trying to have sex and it soon became normal not to. Thankfully, Eoghan was still affectionate towards me; always doling out cuddles and kisses, which to me was the most important thing. But every couple needs sex, don't they? The intimate act, the personal secret which divides you from mates and companions. I worried that we tightroped that fine line between partners and just-best-friends. It all added to the fear that I was being pigeonholed: as Eoghan's carer, not his partner, as a nursemaid and not an equal. He was relying more and more on me but could offer very little back, in physical support. I didn't have enough strength for me, let alone to carry the both of us.

After the doctors suggested his erectile dysfunction

might be psychological instead of physical, I was so worried about mentioning the topic, in case they accused me of unfairly pressurizing him, that the subject of sex soon became taboo between me and Eoghan. As a couple we could talk about anything and everything and yet suddenly there was a no-go area between us. Like an infertile couple who notice every pram, or a dieter who spots every fast-food sign, it seemed to me that everyone was having sex but me.

I'd glare at kissing couples in the street, crumple condom adverts from the centrefolds of magazines and switch television channels at the merest hint of a sex scene. I could act this erratically when it was just me, but when Eoghan was at my side, I had to endure it. Instead, if we were watching a film where the leading couple gets it on, we both blushed and stared down at our hands, trying to ignore the big white elephant which thunders into the room, oddly enough dressed in a garter belt and thigh-high boots.

Everyone's. Having. Sex. But. Us.

I hurl the balled-up words at Eoghan like a hand grenade across the room. But only in my mind, of course, because I'm not allowed to say these things out loud. Don't. Mention. Sex. Or the lack of it.

The doctors have told me, and the doctors rule our lives.

And so to our wedding night. I'm not expecting sex; not naive enough to believe his anatomy will suddenly start functioning because I have a wedding dress on. But Eoghan feels it is his duty. He doesn't want to let me down. Which makes the whole thing ten times worse. He wants to try, so I do my best, trying every trick in the book to get him aroused. But he still can't get hard.

It's four in the morning, and it's been such a long day. I sit on the bed in my 'special' wedding underwear set, chosen to match the ivory of my dress. And Eoghan sits next to me, his head in his hands, looking young, scared and drained. 'I can't even fuck my wife on our wedding night,' he whispers, as a tear runs down his cheek and drops on to the duvet. I reach over to cradle him, but he pushes me away, angry now, frustrated at himself.

'This stupid fucking body,' he cries out, punching his balled fist into a pillow.

'This fucking body won't work for me. What am I meant to do? I just want out of it. I mean, what use am I to you, Amy? You might as well leave me and find someone else who can give you what you need.'

Maybe I should have been more sympathetic, but in fact this barrage only makes me angrier.

'I just married you,' I shriek. Our bridal suite window is wide open, so the partygoers in the courtyard outside must be enjoying quite a show, but I don't care: 'I married you because I love you – more fucking fool me. I changed my life for you, Eoghan.'

He opens his mouth to interrupt, but I'm on a roll, pent-up words belching from the pit of my stomach where they've been fermenting for months.

'No! I didn't just change my life, I stopped it completely. I gave up everything, can't you see that? I moved fucking countries, I left my family. I don't even know if I'll pass my degree. But I had no choice because I love you, and I was never going to walk away from you. So don't tell me to go find someone else now, you selfish bastard. If it was as easy as that I'd have done it a year ago.' For the first time, as I say this, I wish I had. I wish I'd left him. I wish my life was different.

'Do you think I want a wedding day like this?' I ask, tears dripping from my cheek bones and punctuating the words with regret. 'This isn't exactly the wedding day I dreamed of. It's not exactly what I hoped when you asked me to marry you – when you weren't sick and our lives weren't this shit. But I love you, and I'd do anything to make you happy.'

Instantly, I regret my outburst. Why couldn't I have held my tongue for just a few more weeks? What if he dies in the night and the last thing I've done is argue with him?

You see, that's the problem: when your partner is dying you're no longer equal. You can never win an argument, voice a grudge or fall asleep on a cross word, because there may not be a chance to kiss and make up in the morning. And that leaves you in a very weak position. Because, to be absolutely straight with you, most patients aren't as placid as their name suggests: particularly when they're a cancer sufferer riddled by pain or dosed up on morphine. I know Eoghan doesn't mean to be short with me, shout at me or fly off the handle, but when he's shattered from chemo he inevitably does, and as the carer you can only grin and bear it. Like a mother soothing a tantruming child, I'd count to ten and let him cool, because I was terrified he might die in the night and the last voice he'd hear would be a raised one. What sort of send-off would that be for my husband?

Eoghan, however, has no concerns about censoring himself.

'You spoilt little brat,' he explodes. 'You silly fucking child. Grow up.'

'Fuck you,' I yell.

'Fuck you too,' he yells back.

'Oh God, I wish you would,' I flare. Shit, that punch was below the belt.

Silence. In the distance, the local church bells chime like those at the end of a boxing match. Depleted, both fighters slink back to their corners.

This is why, on their wedding night, the new bride and groom sleep in separate rooms. Eoghan pulls the pillows from the bed and sleeps on the couch in the living room of the bridal suite and I cling to a corner of the king-sized bed. Oddly enough, I sleep right through the night, deeply and dreamlessly, as if under anaesthetic. I am happy to give into unconsciousness – sleep is an escape at least.

The next morning – on the first dawn of our honeymoon – I wake to find a cup of tea waiting on the night stand and a foil-covered chocolate in the shape of a heart perched next to it. Eoghan is whistling, merrily, in the other room, a sure sign he is nervous. I know him too well by now.

I cough, loudly, to let him know I'm awake, and a moment later he strolls into the bedroom: 'Good morning, my beautiful wife,' he says, leaning down to kiss me on the forehead. The cuffs of his oversized dressing gown, which hang low over his hands, aren't quite long enough to hide his trembling fingertips. This moment marks a crossroads. I can either gloss over the issue, as Eoghan obviously wants to, or stand my ground and show him my opinion counts.

'Good morning, my wonderful husband,' I reply. 'Shall we go down for some breakfast now?'

We stroll down to breakfast hand in hand, in matching fluffy white dressing gowns, just as we'd seen honeymooners do in movies. The reception staff cheer as we walk past, and one boisterous porter remarks: 'What are you two newlyweds doing out of bed? Don't you have some consummating to do?'

Eoghan, ever the showman, slaps him on the back and says: 'Don't worry about that, mate. My wife is quite satisfied. How do you think I've worked up such an appetite?'

I train my eyes on the floor and feel my heart sink to my feet, as blood rises to my cheeks.

'Eogh, I'm really hungry. Can we go for breakfast?' I mutter, my lips barely moving. I don't want any attention directed at me.

He glances at his blushing bride and gets the hint, quickening our pace through the reception hall. I grip his hand tighter, keep my head bowed and pray that no one else notices us. I drive back from my honeymoon with a neck stiff from staring at the floor.

As for the argument – we never mentioned it again. As for sex – we never had that either. Eoghan was to die three weeks later. So much for the perfect wedding day.

It's unavoidable that these memories contaminate the day I got married, and seeing the DVD leaves me feeling uneasy. I'm glad I watched it once: just to prove I could at least sit through the thing from beginning to end, but I won't be doing it again any time soon.

I'll never be one of those widows who watch their wedding video repeatedly, kissing the television screen and rewinding the best bits. I don't think I'll ever take comfort from it, because the bride and groom, up there on screen, don't even look like me and him.

Eoghan, suited and booted, and me dressed in a veil, none of that is real. If I want to remember my husband, I think of him, fit and well, as he was in Australia: laid flat on his stomach on a surfboard, his arms slicing through the water on either side. Or sitting in a hospital bed, reading a women's magazine and cackling with laughter as he filled in a survey entitled: 'Is your menstrual cycle ruling your life?'

That's my husband – that's how I'd prefer to remember him.

I place the DVD delicately back in its case and put the case in the memory box I have filled with Eoghan keepsakes. I then place the box on top of my wardrobe, right at the back, flat against the wall.

When Eoghan first died I slept with this box on his side of the bed every night. I'd wake in the night and reach out for it, weave my fingers around the ribbons that hinge the base and lid. There was something comforting in its rigidity, in its weight on the mattress, something firm and reassuring that was preferable to an empty space. After moving to London I repositioned the box in my bedside table, then slowly and subtly over the following months, it moved further out of sight and reach. I'm yet to find the perfect spot for it. On top of my wardrobe is not quite right. It's that little too high – a fingerbreadth out of reach. If I want to retrieve it, it proves an uncomfortable stretch.

But I leave it there for now, as I have no other ideas. One day I'll find the perfect balance: a place to store my memories where they're not too overbearing but just within reach.

The fuck-you argument, as we will refer to it, which took place on our wedding night is never mentioned again. It joins the list of subjects that the doctors and our welfare nurse at the hospital have advised me – read *told* me – I'm never to broach. My taboo list now reads: sex, rows and, also, cigarettes.

Yes, cigarettes. Don't. Mention. Cigarettes. Or the reappearance of them.

You'll remember my previously having told you how, when we met in Byron Bay, Eoghan not only gave up alcohol but cigarettes overnight, and how astounded I was that he hadn't touched one since. Well, things have moved on from then.

May bank holiday, 2007

I had started to notice Eoghan acting oddly. Granted, he had just completed a course of high-dose radiotherapy, so I knew to expect some erratic behaviour, but this was different. He was acting – shifty. Suddenly, my fiancé, as he was back then, wanted more independence. He wanted to walk twenty minutes to the village to buy milk, even though there was a petrol station at the end of the road. And what's more he wanted to do it alone – he was quite definite about that. Then, two hours later, he'd be craving some crisps, but the multi-pack of flavours we had wouldn't do. So he'd walk down again. And, again, I was not to go with him.

'Daddy,' I phone home to ask my father's advice: 'He keeps going off on his own. I'm worried, but he isn't opening up to me, which is unlike him. What shall I do?'

'Ame, you have to let him do whatever he feels like,' my father replies. 'He's got a lot to sort through in his head. And a bit of fresh air won't do him any harm.'

The thing is, once Eoghan's chemotherapy started again, he no longer had the energy to endure these daily walks. His thirty-minute hikes turned to five, then stopped completely as the side effects of the drug kicked in and he could no longer walk our garden path without getting out of breath.

'Never mind, Eoghs,' I told him one Sunday, as we tried and failed to negotiate the hilly path that led from our house to the village. 'Now that summer is here and the weather's getting hotter, I'll set up a deckchair for you in the back garden. It'll be just as nice.'

It wasn't a bad substitute, I thought, as I pulled the cobwebbed deckchair from the moth-riddled depths of our garden shed. The garden that circled our studio was quite beautiful: just the right kind of overgrown, with wild herbs and a cherry tree, it was like a fairy's grotto: the perfect place for him to sit and think.

With one last tug I pulled the rear legs of the chair from the garden odds and sods it was anchored to. With it came a blanket of dust and dirt that showered over my head and coated my clothes making me look like a victim of the eruption of Mount Vesuvius.

Coughing and spluttering, yet still holding tight to the

wretched deckchair, I hear laughter from behind me. I turn around to glare at my husband, but as usual his smile is too infectious to outwit and so I laugh with him.

'You look like an eejit,' he spits out between snickers.

I jut my bottom lip out, feigning a sulk.

'Don't give me that. Come here,' he says, moving towards me, his arms outstretched.

Then: 'Fuck me, Ames. What's in that shed? You reek.'

I lift my T-shirt from my stomach, press the fabric to my nose, take a long sniff and catch the aroma of: 'Fertilizer. I smell like shit, literally.'

'I don't care if you stink. I still love you,' Eoghan says, taking an exaggerated breath as if he's about to free dive, then swooping in for a hug. He buries his nose in the crook of my neck and inhales: 'You still smell beautiful, Amox, even when you're covered in poo.'

'OK,' I laugh, prising myself away. 'Time for me to get in the shower.'

For a moment I think he might offer to join me. But that was our old life, our old game. I catch his eye, for a second the sun moves behind a cloud and I wonder if he misses us as much as I do.

By the time I'm showered and dressed he has the deckchair set up in the centre of the grass and is sat legs spread, with his head cocked to one side, staring into the shed. I walk up behind him and place my hand on the crown of his head, stroking the one sprinkling of downy hair that has remained. He tilts his head back and smiles.

'What are you looking so pleased about?' I ask.

'I've got a new project,' he says. 'I'm going to clear out the shed. And before you say anything,' he continues,

'I won't move the big stuff: just organize the shelves and sweep it out. I'll take my time. I won't tire myself out. And I'll wear gloves so I don't pick up any bugs. Come on, Ame, I'd prefer to keep busy.'

What can I say? For the next two days I watch from a distance as he potters around, always wary that he'll do too much and overstretch himself. It comes as a relief when, by midweek, his project is complete.

'Where are you going?' I ask on the Wednesday, as he crosses the garden to the shed's furthest corner. 'I thought you were all done.'

'I am,' he says, 'but I like it in there. Anyway I'm going to practise the meditation you taught me.' He proffers the incense sticks in his right hand as evidence. 'So leave me in peace for a while, OK?'

Three, four times a day, he goes into that shed and closes the door behind him.

I call my father: 'Daddy, he's spending hours in there. I thought he might be crying, but his eyes are never red. What shall I do?'

'Ame, you have to let him do whatever he feels like,' my father repeats. 'He's got a lot to sort through in his head. Let him be.'

But curiosity gets the better of me. And it's so easy to cross a grassy garden in bare feet without being heard. I wrench open the door, and there sits my husband, on an upturned flower pot: eyes wide with guilt and a lit cigarette hanging from the corner of his mouth.

'Fuck,' he says.

I sink to my knees on the grass. My stomach twists into a double helix and, when he moves towards me, tries to reach out and comfort me, I slap him full blown in the face.

'I'm sorry. Fuck: just listen.' He's crying now, and it's not from the sting of my lightweight blow: 'Amy, I know what you're thinking.'

He does, he knows me well enough.

'You think I've given up. That I'm smoking because I'm dying so it won't make a blind bit of difference anyway.'

I'm crying now, because that's it, in its entirety. The point I always feared he'd reach.

'You ask me to trust you,' I say.

'I know.'

'You said you believed you could beat it.'

'I still do.'

'So why are you smoking these fucking things?' I yell, snatching the packet of Marlboros from his pocket and ripping into them, tobacco raining on to the grass around my knees.

The house phone starts ringing.

'You better get that,' I challenge. 'It might be the hospital. Remember them? The people who are wasting their time and money trying to *save you*!'

I watch as Eoghan walks up the garden to the house, his head hung so low I'm surprised he can see where he's going. It is indeed the hospital, confirming the time for his chemo tomorrow. By the time he's finished the phone call my anger has subsided. I just feel defeated. When Eoghan walks back out to the garden I'm busy picking each fleck of cigarette from the soil, tidying the crime scene and erasing the evidence.

He opens his mouth but I'm a second in front: 'Let's not talk about it, Eoghs, all right?'

'If that's what you want.' His relief annoys me. 'But I'm going to speak to the doctors tomorrow and ask them to help me quit, for good this time. I promise I won't ever smoke another cigarette again.'

The next day, Eoghan's in the bathroom, when the doctor asks me for a word.

'Let him have a cigarette if he wants one,' he says. 'Amy, at this stage, it really won't make any difference. And one more thing: it's probably best to avoid the subject. We don't want him getting any more upset, do we?'

Chapter Ten

Rachel has found a lump in her neck – a swollen growth on the left-hand side of her windpipe, the width of two fingertips and the texture of a tumour. Unlike most twenty-four-year-olds, I am, sadly, too familiar with the texture of a tumour. By the time Eoghan died, his skin was dotted with them, and a new one seemed to appear every day, across his chest, down his thighs, in the delicate nape of his neck. Every morning he'd stand naked before me, and I'd ritually rub a cream called Ozonated Gel into each purple-tinged growth, in the banal hope that one day they'd miraculously disappear. I'd bought the Ozonated Gel online, for an atrocious sum of money, from a website that sold alternative medicines and was filled with the testimonies of ex-cancer sufferers who had 'miraculously' recovered after using the cream. I wasn't quite foolish enough to believe them, but at the very least the gel served as a placebo, offering Eoghan and me a glimmer of hope as his chemo continued to fail.

Today, I still keep a half-used pot of Ozonated Gel in my toiletry bag, and every now and then, if my week has gone particularly badly, I unearth it, guiltily unscrew the lid, press the pot to my nostrils, shut my eyes and inhale.

The smell of the cream is quite unique: medicinally sour with an undercurrent of lemon. Instantly I'm back with him, in the living room of our Dalkey apartment, stroking the putty-like gel over his skin, but as soon as I open my eyes the spell is broken. It never helps. I really need to throw the damn pot out.

First thing Monday morning I go with Rachel to her appointment at the hospital, where the doctor fingers her neck and slides a camera up her nostril and down her oesophagus. He immediately schedules her in for a biopsy, with the reassurance that it could be a simple cyst – or Hodgkin's Lymphoma, though this would be the worst-case scenario.

My heart breaks for Rachel as she hears the C-word, and her eyes well up with frightened tears. It's so rare to see her anything but upbeat. She's cheered me up so many times, on my bad days since I've moved into the house, and I desperately want to do the same for her.

I hold her hand and stroke her hair, but can't tell her not to worry as I know there's no comfort in clichés and platitudes. In the taxi home she sits muted and pale, staring out of the rain-speckled window at the smog-stained buildings of the city. I don't disturb her. Right now she is busy; bartering with God and pleading that he'll spare her.

We get back home. Rachel switches on *Coronation Street*. I brew two large mugs of tea, dosed with heaped teaspoons of sugar and a drop of whiskey. She sits on one sofa and I curl up on the neighbouring armchair, idly stroking the felt tassel of a cushion between finger and thumb, for comfort. It's a sombre night and I'm thankful when Rachel excuses herself at 10 p.m. and goes to her bed. As soon as I hear her bedroom door close, I reach for my phone and speed-dial 'home'.

By the time my mum answers on the third ring I am shaking and wailing and completely inconsolable. What's more, I am utterly disgusted with myself because – OK, I admit it – I'm not crying for Rachel. As much as I pity her, she's not who my tears are for. The truth is I resent her: for reminding me of this bastard disease. I'm the one I feel sorry for.

'It's happening again,' I hiccup into the phone. 'This fucking cancer won't leave me alone.'

'It's probably nothing.' My mother tries and fails to calm me down. 'The doctors have to tell you the worst-case scenario, but it's more likely to be a benign tumour or even just glandular fever.'

In that instant I know, deep down in my gut, that Rachel has cancer. Just like I knew with my father and with Eoghan, long before the results were confirmed. Five years before, when Daddy was taken to hospital with shortness of breath, my mother reeled out the same platitudes: 'Don't cry, Amy, your daddy's fit and healthy. And far too young to have anything seriously wrong. He's just been overstretched at work, he's tired, run down, there's no need to worry.'

The same platitudes were repeated for Eoghan: 'Don't cry, Amy, Eoghan's fit and healthy. And far too young to have anything seriously wrong. He's just picked up a chest infection on the long-haul flight, he's tired, run down, there's no need to worry.'

If there's one thing I've learned, it's that people talk shit. Faced with a painful confession, even those you love and trust will lie and take the easy way out. Yes, they do it to spare you, but it won't stop the shit hitting the fan in the end.

Take Eoghan, who, the night before he died, looked me squarely in the eye and promised: 'Trust me, Amy, I'm not going anywhere. I'm not going to leave you; I'm going to give us a future, just trust me.'

Three days later I buried the bastard. So forgive me for being a sceptic.

'Don't cry, Amy, Rachel's fit and healthy. And far too young to have anything seriously wrong. She's been drinking too much alcohol, she's tired, run down, there's no need to worry.'

That's it. Enough! 'SHUT UP!' I scream. 'I've heard all this shit before. Do you think I'm an idiot? Do you know how many times I've heard all this? You told me Daddy's tumours would be benign; you told me Eoghan would be fine, you told me he wouldn't die. Why the fuck should I listen to you, any of you, any more?'

'Amy, calm down.' My mother tries to shush me. 'You can't compare Rachel to Eoghan, or your daddy. It's three totally different things.'

'No it's not,' I sob. 'It's the same thing happening again and again. I'm never going to be free of this nightmare, because this is obviously God's plan for me.'

With hindsight I realize I sounded hysterical, but to me it all made perfect sense.

'That's what I'm here for,' I babble. 'Everyone I love will get cancer and it's my job to care for them until they die, just like I did with my husband.' It all makes sense now, I think. Eoghan was only diagnosed once Daddy was in remission, now Eoghan's died, Rachel's tumour is found. It's all in sequence. It's all mapped out.

'I'm sorry, Mama,' I say aloud. 'I need to go to bed, I'll call you in the morning when I've had time to think.' I hang up before she replies.

I lie in bed, toss and turn with worry. When I realize sleep is out of the question, I do the only thing I can think of and text Tyler.

At midnight he arrives on my doorstep. God knows what lie he's told Hannah. I haven't seen him since the day of the London Marathon, but I'm not too surprised to see him. He seems to have a sixth sense for when I'm at my weakest, and this isn't the first time he's arrived, unannounced, on the days I'm most fragile.

Though my bruises are little more than yellowed blotches now, I can't forgive him as quickly. He smells of cheap lager and undercooked burgers, which tells me he's been on a boys' night out, and when he kisses me my gag reflex twitches – so why don't I push him away?

I am exhausted from the day's upheaval. I don't bother to protest as Tyler walks into my bedroom and automatically unbuttons his trousers. He already has a hard-on, and I wonder if he masturbates in the car outside to make his visit to me as fleeting as possible. I switch off the bedroom light so he can't see my lifeless expression as he fucks me, and manoeuvre into the doggy position, knowing this will get it over with more quickly. As he comes I whisper: 'Do you love me, do you love me?'

He groans as he empties himself into me and says: 'Yeah, I love you, fuck me, you're amazing, Amy.' Already he is reaching for a tissue, pulling on his T-shirt, cleaning himself up before he goes back to his betrothed. I lie on my stomach, naked on the bed, and wonder why I put myself through this.

He crosses the room and, crouching to my eye level, kisses me gently on the tip of the nose, then says: 'You're beautiful, Ams. I'll see you some time soon.' He strokes my hair and says, 'I love you.'

Those three simple words: so soothing to hear when your heart is broken and bruised. He knows, with those words, he's got me tethered.

The next day I wake up and throw up. The following morning the same happens, and the next and the next. On day four Rachel's test comes back negative. On day five I wake and feel fine again.

Looking back on my hysterical reaction to Rachel's close call, I wonder: am I addicted to drama? Am I so used to living on the edge that life without trauma now bores me? Since I was eighteen years old, my life has run like a soap opera: I've sat with my father through three years of chemotherapy, got engaged in a whirlwind romance and then, to top it all off, my husband died on me. Now, for the first time in years, there are no ripples on the water and yet I'm more restless than ever.

Ironically, when I was a teenager, I often used to fantasize about a loved one dying: sometimes it would be my mum or dad, and other times I'd kill off a make-believe boyfriend. In my fantasy, friends and family would flock around me, showering me with love and sympathy. I was a typical teenager crying out for attention. The sad thing is, I already had parents who doted on me. From childhood I was the apple of my father's eye, and my mother and I were carbon copies of each other. Yet, as a teenager, I was still bitterly jealous of my older sister, Louise, who was an A-star student and gold-medal athlete. The attention I got was never enough, compared to the accolades she earned.

I once heard my mum on the phone to a schoolfriend, whom she hadn't seen in years, talking about my sister and me.

'Louise is three years older than Amy,' she explained. 'She was a dream to bring up: a daydreamer, yes, but mature and sensitive. She never caused us any trouble.

'But with Amy, God obviously had other plans. Yes, she's fiercely bright, just like her sister, but they're galaxies apart in temperament. Amy's always been the same: highly entertaining, artistic, borderline eccentric, and an absolute attention-seeker.' She said none of this with any malice, it was merely an observation that everyone in the family agreed upon.

By the time Eoghan died I couldn't have been more different to the teenager who would stamp her feet if all eyes weren't on her. My response to Eoghan's death was quite different to the grief I'd imagined. I didn't want attention, quite the opposite, in fact, and from the day of the funeral, when all the formalities were done, I simply shut myself away.

I'd always had an affectionate nature, but suddenly the thought of someone hugging me made me cringe. I couldn't bear to be touched, mollycoddled or even spoken to. If friends came to visit I'd crouch behind the cabinets in the kitchen pretending I wasn't at home. When my parents flew over on visits from England I'd scarcely be able to breathe until I knew they were back on that plane – a safe distance away. I only wanted Eoghan, and if he couldn't come to me, I was determined to go to him.

3 July 2007

I began to plan my suicide the day after Eoghan dies. I remember telling my father quite calmly: 'I've asked Eoghan if he'll come and get me.'

I can't imagine how it punctured his heart to hear his younger daughter say she wanted to die but, to give them credit, neither of my parents tried to change my mind. Instead my dad went on a long walk, and later confessed that he'd sat on the wall of the nearby harbour and cried and begged for God to help me. He asked the angels to help me to live or die: whichever would bring me some peace.

Five days later my parents had no choice but to fly back to London – they had jobs to return to, bills to pay and lives to continue. For the first time since Eoghan's death I was alone in our apartment. And God, it was such a relief to be by myself, without the suffocating barrage of sympathy and condolences. I sat on the sofa with my feet neatly tucked under me. I brushed my hair and did my make-up. On the arm of the sofa, I lined up forty sleeping pills, perfectly in a row. I sat and looked at them for a while. I scooped them into my palm and held them a centimetre in front of my eye. I sniffed them – they smelled of talcum powder and creosol. I took a spoon from the kitchen and crushed the little white pellets into a fine powder. I planned to snort them, one line of powder after another, in quick succession.

But – what do you know? – when it came down to it, I couldn't. Possibly it's because I'm a coward, or possibly it's because I'm braver then I ever realized, because my overriding thought that moment was: How can I do this when Eoghan fought so hard to stay alive?

I think back to that day in Easkey, when I told Eoghan I planned to commit suicide if he died. I hear his voice, as clear as if he were still in the room saying: 'If you choose to die you will destroy your parents' lives; you'll kill your sister, your cousins and your grandparents. They'll never forgive themselves. And I tell you now, Amy, I will never ever forgive you. If you want to do that then fine, go jump off a building, but I won't be waiting for you.'

I sat there for what felt like days, but in reality was probably less than an hour. My mind had been made up long before I crushed up the sleeping pills. Part of me knew I'd never go through with it. I promised Eoghan, you see. And I'd never let him down.

In the end I brushed the granular powder into the woven tapestry of the carpet, then the next day vacuumed it clean away. I never considered suicide again, and when times were really tough it didn't even occur to me. I'm stubborn like that – once I make up my mind, I don't look back. But it sickens me that I got so close. What a waste of a life it would have been.

So you see, I've had quite enough drama in my life for now but, to be honest, I do sometimes miss living on the edge. The view from there takes your breath away.

I like to keep my life simple these days, and my past and present compartmentalized. I don't have much evidence of my husband on show, just three favourite photos of him on my wall, but I hide even these when Tyler drops by.

These pictures have been stuck to the wall and then unstuck so many times that the corners are transparent where the backing paper has been pulled off by the Blu-tack. Eoghan's photos invite questions – questions I'm in no rush to answer, and the last thing I want to see, when I'm straddling one man, is my husband's face, smiling encouragement. This is why, although Tyler has known me for months, he has no idea what my elusive husband looks like. He never asks and I never offer details about my past. In return, I don't ask questions about Hannah. I'm not the type of Other Woman who Googles her name, finds where she works, and then lurks on the periphery of her building, waiting for a glimpse of their rival.

I have a sneaking suspicion Hannah and I are probably polar opposites – because isn't that why men have mistresses, so they can have their cake and eat, not only a slice of Victoria sponge, but also of Black Forest gateau? I imagine she is dark-haired and curvy: weighs a stone more then me, but carries it well, on her arse and full bust. I bet she is 'nice' in that 'If I found an injured bird I would nurse it back to health' sort of way that I will never be – I'm more likely to have run over the damn bird in the first place. I am sure she mothers him, because every man secretly wants that in a partner – cooks for him, and irons his trousers with a perfectly crisp line down the seams. By having two of us, he ticks all the boxes. She is his cook in the kitchen, just as I am his whore in the bedroom. If we had the same winning attributes the affair would be pointless. I don't need to meet her to know her. I just look at myself, reverse the image and there she is.

Oddly enough, the same applies to Tyler and Eoghan,

looks wise. Eoghan's foppish blond hair could not be compared to Tyler's closely cut dark crop, or his taut muscled body to Tyler's slightly convex belly. Even the tint of their skin is different, but this can't be surprising with two men from contrasting Irish and Italian gene pools. Anyway, my point is, Tyler doesn't know this, because he's never seen a picture of Eoghan – until today.

I didn't know Tyler was coming round, so didn't have time to pull the photos of Eoghan off the wall before he walked into my bedroom. OK, that's not perfectly true – I could have made time. When I peered out of the basement window and saw it was Tyler stabbing the doorbell with his forefinger, I could have dashed into my room on the way to open the front door. I could have ripped them off their adhesive and stuffed them in my knicker drawer, as I've always done before. But I didn't. Now I wonder why not. Why, on that day, did I want my two worlds to collide? Simply, I just wanted to see what would happen.

Tyler didn't notice them at first. He is a man, after all, and whereas most women scan every room they enter out of habit, most men are tragically unobservant. Also, his mind was on one thing – the purpose of this unscheduled visit – which was to have sex with me and get home as quickly as possible because Hannah would have his tea on the table. By now I'm well trained and get obediently into his favourite position, flat on my back with my head hung back over the side of the bed. It gives me a crick in my neck. Thankfully, he doesn't bother to overexert himself and comes quickly, without trying to prolong the procedure. It's as he stands to wipe himself down that he sees the photographs. I'm sitting on the bed, after uprighting myself, my back rested against a bundle of pillows, sleepily watching him, wondering how long I can carry this on, when I see the muscles in his neck twitch as he spots the photos and realizes who this other man must be.

He asks the question anyway, although there could only be one answer.

'Who're those pictures of?'

'Eoghan.'

'Oh.'

Tyler, a man who can talk himself into or out of any given situation, is suddenly at a loss for words.

Then: 'He looks so young.'

'He was.'

'He looks so well.'

'He was, once.'

'Were they taken long before . . . you know?'

'Around six weeks.'

'Oh.'

I have an urge to grab the photos, rip them up, and eat the pieces. Hide the evidence and hope this awkwardness disappears with them, because Tyler's staring, transfixed by the photographs, and I can sense something between us shifting. He's thinking of me differently. He no longer sees me alone, but Eoghan and me as one entity: the hand-cuffed couple I've been trying to extricate myself from.

'Ty, are you OK?' I ask. 'I can take the photographs down. It's really no big deal. I didn't mean to make you uncomfortable.'

'No, it's fine,' he replies in a voice an octave too high for me to believe him.

'You did know about Eoghan,' I press. 'It's not like

you're just finding out I was married. I explained all this, when we first got together. This isn't the first you've been told about him.'

He peels his eyes off the pictures, to turn and look at me. 'I know,' he says. 'I just didn't know he was so . . . normal.'

Even though we're told, in the media, in public-health announcements and in charity campaigns, that cancer can hit us and kill us at any age, we prefer to imagine the cancer victim as a middle-aged man who smoked thirty a day and was heading for a coronary anyway. I had my reality check when my dad, a non-smoker and practically a tee-totaller, was diagnosed, but some lucky people can still convince themselves it 'wouldn't happen to me'.

'I did know his age, but I thought he'd be older,' Tyler says, and though his words are nonsensical on paper, they do make sense, to me. He was expecting a face warped with ill health, the mark of a man who hadn't looked after himself. That would be easier to understand than the 'face of cancer' being a healthy, vibrant young man.

I have the same response from people when they hear my story through the grapevine and then go on to meet me. They're told at the offset, 'She was twenty-three,' but then they hear the word 'widow' and it adds fifty years to my age, instantly. 'Widow' means pensioner or, at least, a middle-aged mother of 2.4 kids. To be widowed in your twenties is unfortunate, uncomfortable and, we like to believe, unlikely. I'm a walking, talking reality shock. As are those photographs of Eoghan.

'He looks happy,' says Tyler.

'He was. We were: nearly all of the time,' I answer.

'You loved him.' It's not a question, this time, but a declaration, as if Tyler's only just realized.

'Yes.' The admission hurts: pulled from me, like a rotting tooth. 'I did love him. I still do love him.'

Tyler nods slowly. I can hear his brain whirring, to process this abundance of new information. Oddly, I think of the Etch-a-Sketch I had when I was a kid. I'd spend hours drawing out an overlapping tangle of aluminium lines, then simply shake the board and the screen would be perfectly clear again, to start afresh. If only people were that simple. And, if I shook Tyler hard enough, I would wipe his mind clean again. Hell, I'd do the same for myself.

'Tyler,' I say, forcing my voice to sound teasing. I need to splinter this silence, and we only have one common ground: 'Come and lie with me on the bed.' I reach out and stroke his arm, but he shrugs me off and moves a step further away. Further away from me and nearer to the pictures, which I'm going to tear to threads in a minute if he doesn't stop staring at them. Fuck, I can't handle this. I'm out of my depth. I can always appease Tyler with sex. I don't have much else to offer. If he no longer wants to shag me, I'll have no value to him.

'Tyler,' I try again, 'come and sit next to me, won't you?'

He sighs, as if he's exasperated by my interruption into his thoughts, turns his wrist as if to look at the time, but it's an unconvincing gesture, seeing as his watch is still on my bedside table, where he propped it during foreplay.

'It's late, I should get going.'

I'm thankful now that he's leaving. With my husband, my lover and me in the bedroom there's no space to breathe.

I walk him to the door and lean, as always, to kiss him on the lips, but he turns his head, out of range, before turning my face to kiss me, politely, on the cheekbone.

'Thank you for having me over. It was nice to see you,' he says, as if thanking his aged neighbour for inviting him in for Sunday dinner. 'I hope the rest of your week at work goes OK.'

'Huh,' I grunt, unable to think of a more appropriate response. I walk back into my bedroom, and sit on the edge of my bed, on top of my hands to stop them shaking.

What happens when your two worlds collide? Well, it seems that one man has to bow out, gracefully, because with three it's just too uncomfortably crowded.

I hear Tyler's van pull out of my driveway; the engine revs and then grows quieter as he rallies down the road and around the corner on to the high street. I suspect I will never see him again. Not in this sense anyway. I may run into him occasionally, on a Friday night when our paths overlap, but it will never be the same.

I feel no sense of loss that our affair is ending. If anything, I feel relieved. Because sex I can do. I've proved it: we've done it, and that's all Tyler and I ever can be. It's time I looked for more than that.

Chapter Eleven

For weeks now I've known something is wrong – correction: very wrong – with my life. I haven't known exactly what, until today, but I've known that very soon something would need to shift and change. The beauty about having a dead husband watching over you is that I trust he will send me a sign if my life is heading off track. In the last year I've grown accustomed to Eoghan's 'signs' and have learned how to read them. It starts as a gut feeling, a nagging concern that something is awry. Next it's the dreams: the same repetitive scenario, night after night, leaving me ill at ease in the morning.

For the last week I've had the same dream every night. I'm swimming, front crawl, up and down the length of a swimming pool. There's no water in the pool, but shredded paper mottled with ink spots. There are typewritten words on the paper, but I can't stop to read them and I don't know who wrote them. My family line up on the edge of the pool, watching me swimming. When I notice them there I want to up my pace, to prove I'm stronger than they give me credit for, but I feel like I'm swimming through treacle. As the dream drifts on I grow tired, achingly weary; however,

I know I can't stop until I count a hundred lengths. My father tells me to rest, but I can't.

'You don't understand. I always swim one hundred lengths,' I tell him. 'I can't stop now.' I know that if I stop swimming now something very bad will happen. I don't know what, the dread is unspecified, but I feel its familiar pull.

Each night a different member of my family steps forward to say: 'What's happened to you, Amy? You've changed since he left you. You used to be fun. You used to be joyful. If only Eoghan was here to help you.'

I cry as I swim and, because dreams are limitless, I scream and laugh all at once. And because dreams don't judge you, I at last admit how I'm feeling.

'I miss him,' I yell into the depths of the pool, the words forming white wash on the surface of the water. 'I'm so fucking lonely. But that's not the worst of it. I'm relieved.' There, I've said it. 'I don't want him back. I'm relieved that he's dead. Yes, I'm thankful he's gone. Because mostly I'm terrified – of ever going back there: of caring for him and dreading the end.'

I look up to the poolside where my family still stand, and wait for their judgement, but their faces are blank. Literally, I can't tell who is who or where each person begins and ends. They just can't understand, I think.

I let myself sink, face first, into the water, too tired to stay afloat any longer. Everything goes quiet.

At this point, every night, I wake up with a start and then, every single time, run to the toilet and shit out my guts. Diarrhoea shoots out of me, and I'm glad. I need to be cleansed. I want to be new and clean again.

* * *

It's Sunday afternoon, and I've just come back from a depressingly mundane blind date with an architect who's a friend of Rachel's. My heart wasn't in it from the start, but I thought I should really give it a go. We'd spoken on the phone once, swapped lighthearted emails and seemed compatible enough on paper, but an hour into the date it was obvious something was missing. That spark, that elusive chemistry. It just wasn't there, and there's no way of manufacturing that.

I could have stuck around and given him a chance, but I don't. Because I'm simply tired of trying so hard, trying to act like everyone else when inside I feel so different. I'm tired of pretending the last few years didn't happen. And so I make an excuse and ditch him. I don't feel too well, I say – it's a painfully obvious fib and I know I come across as rude, but I'm too disheartened to stick around. He walks me to the nearest tube station, kisses my cheek, tells me to go home and rest, and that he hopes I feel better soon. He watches me dodge through the turnstile and turn into the tunnel for the Northern Line. I turn back to wave, in time to see him raise a one-fingered salute at my back. Charming.

I'm not ready to go home and admit my failure to the girls just yet, so take the tube to Camden. It's a relief to be in the hustle and bustle of the market, where visitors are so eclectic that no one stands out from the crowd. I stroll around the stalls, then head to the lock, stopping at the canalside and resting my elbows on the railing. I spend an idle ten minutes staring across the murky water, plotting the voyage of a floating cider bottle en route from a sewage pipe that runs into the river. Then, bored of this game, I people-watch instead.

I spy on a smiling couple, walking hand in hand across the metal bridge that twins the canal sides. I eavesdrop on a group of friends who are trying to think of a way to sneak a bottle of vodka into a nightclub that evening. I watch one lone girl, around the same age as me, savouring a soft-scoop ice cream festooned with rainbow sprinkles. I watch her for almost twenty minutes, from the first lick of her ice cream to the bite she takes from the cone's sodden end. The charm around her neck reads 'Holly', and is definitely only gold-plated, the pink varnish on her nails is chipped and her hair falls raggedly from its ponytail but, with these imperfections, she is happy. She's unguarded, in a way that only comes with youth. In the way that I, at twenty-four, should be too. But still my instinct is to pity her. To assume I have more control of my life than her. 'Does she not have anything more important to do than this today?' I say to myself. Should she not be working, in the gym, or at least meeting friends? I'm so much more productive for being teetotal: without all that silliness, the stupid situations I got myself into before. I'm in control now – I have rules and regulations. My life is ordered again: minus drink and minus men, who just confused things before.

My attention is caught by the couple I was watching before. They've stopped four feet from me, at the gate to the lock, so it's hardly voyeurism; I can't easily avoid them. He whispers something in her ear, she tosses her head back and laughs, and he kisses her neck.

'Huh,' I tut. 'You just wait, love. It's all fun and games now, but don't get too used to having him around.

Nothing's permanent in this lifetime and it's going to sting when he burns you.'

She turns, and he kisses the tip of her nose. I lipread his 'I love you' and see her blush with pleasure. More fool them; I'm better on my own. I'm just fine: much more even-minded, with my strong will to rely on.

She's cold – she shivers and rubs her hands in front of her. He unzips his jacket, pulls her into the folds and wraps it around both of them. They're laughing. They don't even notice the crowds pushing past them. So wrapped up in each other. Honeymoon period probably. In six months they'll be arguing, despising each other. No, much better to be single. Much better to be on my own. I'm definitely right on this one.

Then why am I crying? I barely notice the tears rolling down my cheek. And why does my chest ache as I watch them? I know I don't miss my husband. I don't miss my marriage. I don't miss the hospital, the bad news, the goodbye. But I do miss someone. The Eoghan of before. Who loved me, but didn't need me to mother him. I miss what we had before the cancer distorted it.

I always wanted to prove I wasn't a victim and that the cancer hadn't won. I may not have had my husband, but that was a small obstacle I could overcome. I don't think I've done badly. Look at me now: I have a job on a national newspaper, one that in my university days I would have given my right arm for, and an independent lifestyle that means I no longer need to rely on anyone for anything. I'm in control again. If only I could get rid of Tyler permanently. But I'm working on that.

Since Eoghan died I've been striving for this, fighting

to prove I've lost nothing and determined to show that I'm still someone. But, all this time, have I been fighting for the wrong things?

I realize I can't remember the last time I had fun. My quest for perfection has taken away all the good times. My days are as regimented as the British Army. I live by routine and I'm terrified to break the pattern. Everything I do is a mission. I got the job of my dreams, but I'm miserable because I'm not progressing fast enough. I'm working myself into the ground: hunting for a promotion and a pay rise. I go to the gym every day, sometimes twice, but where's the joy? It's all a chore.

If Eoghan were to meet me now, I fear he wouldn't look twice. He'd look me up and down and say: 'You take yourself far too seriously, Amy. Crack a smile, why don't you?'

He wouldn't date me, and he certainly wouldn't marry me. Everything he loved me for – my energy and optimism and sense of mischief – is fading. It's been replaced with an outward arrogance that actually hides my uncertainty.

Eoghan used to say that the most wonderful thing about me was how much pleasure I got from the tiniest things: like climbing into bed between freshly laundered sheets, or the spicy taste of a chai latte drunk from a china cup. I loved these simple treats. I'd close my eyes and groan with pleasure whilst Eoghan would laugh and laugh and say: 'That's why I love you, Moxy.'

Last night I put clean sheets on my bed, dressed in fresh pyjamas and scrubbed my face with tea-tree oil. I burnt a stick of cider wood – Eoghan's favourite incense – and tried to breathe deeply, but the frown lines in my forehead just wouldn't loosen.

After an hour spent tossing and turning, I can't stay in bed any longer. Like a sleepwalker, I slip out from under the covers and, without processing what I'm doing, go to the edge of my wardrobe and stretch to reach down my memory box from on top. I know what I'm looking for, though I'm not sure how I'm hoping it will help me. There – Eoghan's mobile phone, sandwiched between the worn leather folds of his wallet. I can remember the password, 0105, the day and month of his birth. As the phone powers into life, I have a fleeting thought that going through his inbox might unearth some nasty surprises. If I find out he was having an affair now, I think, I'm going to fucking kill him – again. But his inbox is full to its capacity with texts from me.

28/05/07: Missing you, baby. Wish you were back at home with me, but at least the docs will make sure you don't do a runner and jilt me at the altar. Love you. I'm counting the hours until our big day.

03/06/07: I love you too, with all my heart, and can't wait to marry you. Tomorrow will be the best day of our lives, and I promise it will only get better after that.

04/06/07: I know it's bad luck to see you this morning, but is it jinxing it to text? Anyway, I had to say, I Love You. Also, don't forget to take four steroids before breakfast.

The list goes on, but I don't read any further. However, just as I'm about to switch the phone off, I spot the icon for the mobile's outbox. I wonder if he saved his sent texts as well. There are only three outgoing messages on the phone. One is to his best man, sent on 28 April, asking if he could pick my parents up from the airport when they fly over for the wedding. The other is to his brother: a typically bad and lurid joke he'd forwarded. The third is to my father, sent on 30 June, two days before Eoghan died:

> All right, me old matey [it reads]. Feeling 100 per cent today. Had a great sleep, scoffed a big bowl of porridge plus pancakes and didn't even puke. Your beautiful daughter is looking after me well. Just don't know what I'd do without her. But do me a favour, Stevo, will you check she's OK? She's still only a baby. She needs someone to look after her. I'm no help right now, but she'll talk to you. You have to tell her, whatever happens, to cut herself some slack.

I can hear him say it, crystal clear. I can hear his accentuation on 'cut' and how his voice raises an octave on the vowel of 'slack'. I know this, mainly, because he'd said the same to me a thousand times when he was alive: when I was working until 4 a.m. trying to finish my dissertation, or making multiple phone calls to consultants in England trying to get him accepted on to an obscure medical trial.

'Cut yourself some slack, Amox,' he'd say repeatedly,

until I'd heard them so often the words lost their meaning, and though I'd nod he knew I'd ignored him.

In the end, he pinned a note to our bathroom mirror. This was a traditional place for us to leave notes. When Eoghan's post-breakfast vomiting was at its worst, and he'd spend most of the morning with his head held over the sink, I'd wedge love letters and jokes under the mirror frame, to give him something new to focus on. Each day the notes would change: cartoons cut from comic books, football articles or self-penned love letters. I tried to make them as varied as possible.

One morning, in the short period between our honeymoon and Eoghan's death, I opened the door of the bathroom to find the entire mirror covered in squares of notebook paper, pieced together with tape like a quilted bedspread. Across the paper was a collage of typeface, all capital letters cut from magazines and newspapers.

'Cut yourself some slack,' the ransom note shouts and then, underneath in handwritten biro, 'You can't do it all. Give yourself a break.'

I trace the outline of each letter as I brush my teeth. The bristles of my toothbrush catch my gums and I taste blood. I take a swig of water directly from the cold tap, swish out my mouth and spit a pool of foamy lather into the basin. White saliva swirls into red, red swirls into white and both disappear down the plughole. If only I could follow them.

But I'm not ready to admit defeat just yet.

'I *can* do it all,' I think. 'There'll be enough time to rest when it's over.'

I reread the text from Eoghan to my father:

'You have to tell her, whatever happens, to cut herself some slack.'

This time I don't bother with a poster, as I know from past experience that motivational signs I stick to my wall are far too easy to avoid. Instead I grab a thick black marker, the type you use on whiteboards in school, and jot six words across my wrist joint:

Eoghan Says Cut Yourself Some Slack.

For work on Monday I will write it smaller, in thin scrawls of biro. For months I will write this phrase on my arm with such regularity it soon becomes part of my wake-up routine between washing my face and straightening my fringe.

It seems absurd that something as small as a doodle could mark the turning point in my grief. If this story was fictional, the widow's turning point would be much more dramatic: a moment of utter epiphany, climaxing with Eoghan appearing from the mirror like a spectre. I do apologize if you feel let down.

I'm sorry I can't make this moment more colossal. I did weigh up adding some supernatural activity, to liven things up in the name of art. But then I thought, I've got this far: now is not the right time to exaggerate things.

So I'm sorry, again, if you feel disappointed. I would love to strap some bells and whistles on to my U-turn. Pretend I was visited by angels who set me on the path to enlightenment – or that I fell in love again and remarried.

For those following this story, I'm sure both of these options would be much more gratifying.

Except, in grief, sometimes the most unexpected things can be the most comforting. For me, it was a scribble which curved around my wrist like a bracelet. And the eventual realization that the worst was now behind me and I needed to make sure it stayed there.

As the calligraphy dries on my skin, I start to feel different. The ink is bright blue, like the alkaline tip of a litmus paper, and as it seeps into my bloodstream it seems to neutralize the acidity of my grief. I feel calmer, more neutral: more normal. Normal. Now there's an adjective I never thought I could come close to again.

And still things shift.

The next morning, for the first time in nine weeks, I don't go to the gym. My alarm trumpets into life at 6.15 as usual, and my gym bags are packed and ready by the door, but although my legs twitch regimentally for me to get out of bed and get going, instead I dig my fisted hands under the pillow and force myself to lie there, quite still.

My head screams like an army corporal: 'Get up, you lazy waste of space,' but above it an Irish voice says, quite calmly: 'Lie there for just one more hour, Amy. Nothing will happen if you rest there a while. The sky won't cave in and no one will die. Be kind to yourself. You've punished yourself enough.'

I touch the fingertips of my left hand to my right wrist; close my eyes and fall back to sleep.

I wake up ninety minutes later, dress slowly and deliberately, and still get to the office forty minutes early. To the average person it's a tiny step, but to me it's progress, and for the first time in weeks a genuine smile graces my face.

That evening, instead of going for a swim, I meet Rachel for a glass of wine after work. No more deprivation, I think. There's no harm in a glass of wine. I look down at my wrist – no, Eoghan would firmly agree – and when Rachel and I raise our glasses in cheers, I swear I hear three glasses clink.

The next evening, instead of going for a 10k run as I'd planned, I detour into Waterstones, buy a trashy paperback novel and sit under a blossoming tree on Islington Green. As the sun sets I drift off to sleep, and in my dreams I'm back with him.

27 May 2007

We're in our apartment in Dalkey. It's the end of May and the garden is in full bloom: the outside walls of the studio are webbed with roses, and the cherry tree, overloaded with fruit, casts shade across a lawn specked with daisies. It's a beautiful setting.

It's a shame, then, about the cloud on the horizon. No matter how strong the wind, this one cloud won't shift: Eoghan will die in five weeks' time.

I have to hand my university dissertation in the next day: the deadline is at midday, so I'm catching an eight o'clock flight from Dublin to Heathrow, driving an hour to my university in Southampton, then jumping straight back on to a flight to Dublin. I am all too aware that Eoghan can't be left alone for long. When Eoghan was first diagnosed, my university lecturers predicted it would be almost impossible for me to pass my degree whilst also caring for him, but somehow I did it, in spite of their pessimism. And now my final dissertation is laid out before me on the kitchen table, just waiting to be bound.

The bonus of living in a tiny studio apartment is that, wherever I am, Eoghan – currently dozing in our double bed – is always in view. So, as I put the finishing touches to my dissertation, I keep one eye on his chest rising and falling, to ensure he's still breathing. He's not in a good way today: he's been excruciatingly constipated for three weeks now and is in constant pain. He hasn't slept through the night in weeks and is so drained his face looks almost opaque. He gets more confused each day now, as the tumour in his brain swells, but I pretend I don't notice. There's no use in scaring him when there's nothing we can do to save him.

I tiptoe across the room and crouch beside the bed. His breathing is ragged, but when I feel his forehead his temperature is, thankfully, normal. Suddenly, he opens his eyes and stares at me.

'You OK, baby?' I ask, touching a kiss on to the end of his nose with my fingertips.

His brow furrows. Then 'Who the fuck are you?' he snaps.

I'd been warned to expect it, that one day he may wake up and not even know me. I had just prayed it wouldn't be quite so soon. Cold with shock, I don't even have time to gather myself before he's out of bed, pushing past me, knocking me to the ground.

'Eoghan,' I cry out. 'What are you doing?'

It's clear he doesn't know who he is or what he's doing. He crashes into the arms of the sofa, knocks over a stool, stumbling on his feet like he's had a skinful.

'I've got to get out,' he murmers. 'It's time for me to go.'

He climbs on to the couch – the sheer effort of lifting his legs makes it look like a monumental task. The kitchen table is directly behind the couch, with the pages of my dissertation meticulously laid out, in order, waiting to be filed. I can see what's going to happen, even before Eoghan mounts the back of the couch. I grab his waist from behind to pull him back, but he swings out with his fists and lands a blow to the side of my face.

For a dying man, he packs quite a punch, and I'm knocked off balance, falling into an armchair.

I watch as Eoghan climbs on to the kitchen table, crumpling my work beneath his bare feet, pulls his underpants down to his ankles, squats over the largest pile of papers on the table and takes a shit. That's right – he literally takes a dump. And then, seemingly satisfied, he climbs calmly down from the table and gets back into bed, leaving a coiled pile of excrement on top of the thesis I've worked my arse off to finish before my deadline.

Then he falls asleep – the first time I've seem him sleep soundly for weeks. I fetch a bin bag from the cupboard under the sink, sweep the ruined dissertation, dump and all into the bag and throw it in the bin outside. Then I resignedly sit back at my laptop to reprint almost two hundred pages of work. I don't sleep at all that night.

Every hour the bruise on my face darkens and my heart sinks further. Eoghan, on the other hand, sleeps right through the night, and when I go to wake him the next morning I instantly see that a rosy hue has returned to his cheeks. I stroke the downy hair on his head to wake him. He opens his eyes and smiles.

'Moxy,' he says cheerfully. 'Where are you off to?'

'I'm just flying to London to hand in some coursework,' I tell him. 'I'll be back this evening, and a district nurse will come round at lunchtime to give you your medicine.'

'OK, babe.' He's quite content, oblivious to the previous day's events: 'But what did you do to your cheek? It's bruised.'

'I'll tell you later,' I reply, and make a swift exit before he also spots the tears in my eyes.

This is how it is for the last few weeks of his life: one day he'll be fine and can laugh and joke, completely on the ball, and then the next day he's unreachable. He doesn't remember these bad days, but they're engraved for ever on my soul. I did tell him about the time he shat on the table. And do you know what? The bastard actually laughed: he thought it was hilarious, and phoned his friends to tell them. I laughed along with him. I don't know why.

I'm sitting on my bedroom floor, sorting through some paperwork, when I find a letter from Eoghan's doctor, written in June 2007. It is a referral letter, which I was meant to send on to a consultant at the Royal Marsden Hospital in London, where I was taking Eoghan for a second opinion. The reason I still have it is because Eoghan died two days before we were due to fly to London for the appointment. Sod's law.

I haven't seen this letter in a year, but can still recite it word for word.

'Eoghan Molloy was diagnosed with malignant melanoma in November 2006,' it says: 'Eoghan is a very unfortunate young man. For him there is little hope.'

I was given that letter one day midway through chemo, by a well-meaning nurse who probably didn't know the damning prognosis it contained. She was just the messenger, after all. She handed it to me in an unsealed envelope, as if it were nothing more menacing than a greetings card, and asked me to check if it contained everything I needed. Eoghan was standing right next to me, but was mercifully distracted by a football match playing on the day ward's TV. The first time I read it I barely took it in. The second time, back at home, locked in the toilet, I cried as if my heart was breaking. But, by the third time I read it – whilst Eoghan was in the bath that evening – I was angry. They can call my husband sick, say he's terminal and close to death's door, but never, ever, unfortunate. Just that morning on the way to the hospital, Eoghan had turned to me and said, quite sincerely, 'I'm a lucky bugger, Moxy. Look what I have: the love of my life right by my side. I couldn't ask for anything more. I married the woman I love. I've nothing else left to do.'

If you'd asked Eoghan if he thought himself unfortunate he'd have said you were insane. He thought he was the luckiest man in the world.

That was my husband. And that's why I stood by him. Today, if people hear my story, they tell me I'm brave and loyal but, sadly, I'm really not that heroic. I just happened to fall in love with a wonderful man, who taught me to make the most of every second.

After reading the letter that day, I sit down and write to Eoghan's mum for the first time in months. I tell her I am sorry I couldn't save her son. That I did all I could but I feel in my heart he wasn't meant to survive. It wouldn't suit his spirit – growing old and frail. Eoghan was a man designed to live fast and die young.

'I'm sorry,' I write, 'but I can't feel guilty any more. I loved him and gave him everything. And now it's time to stop picking the wound and let myself heal.'

I have no reason to write this letter. Eoghan's mother never blamed me – quite the opposite, she has always thanked me for taking such good care of him – but I need to write it for myself. I hope that if I see it in black and white I might start to believe it.

Last night I had a tasteless one-night stand. I know I said that was all in the past but, in my defence, I didn't know it was a one-night stand at the time. It wasn't my fault, I was taken advantage of. He said that I was special – yes, in hindsight, it sounds quite obvious now. But as he pulled my dress over my head, and whistled in approval, I really thought this one would want to see me again. Why do I always fall for this tosh?

It was his arms that did it. They were just so strong: so swollen with muscles that, with my two hands cupped around them, my first fingers and thumbs were nowhere

near touching. I met him – Christian, an Australian elec-
trician – at the Old Queen's Head on a particularly raucous
night with Rachel. Twirling on the dance floor, I slipped
and spun right into him. He caught me, and kissed me,
with no pause for conversation. As he kissed me, with his
arms hooked around my waist, he lifted me clean from
the floor. It was at that point that he had me: hook, line
and sinker.

Christian slept at mine that night, but I promise I did
not have sex with him. I swore the same thing to my mum
the next day, when I phoned home to tell her, in simpering
detail, about the perfect new man I was hoping to date.

I'm a reformed character now. The red light above
my bedroom window has been permanently put out. But
God it's nice to have Christian in my bed. He doesn't
let me out of his arms all night. Even when I roll over
to reach for a glass of water, he pulls me back down to
him, protesting: 'Where you going? Come back to me.'
I wake, on the hour every hour, through the night, and
each time we're entwined in a new position, but never
with more than an inch between us. As he stirs in his
sleep, he pulls me closer. I let myself think: 'This one
does like me.'

I'm proud, and mostly surprised, that my willpower
holds out. We kiss and fondle and fumble around, but I
wake the next morning with the cotton shorts of my
pyjamas still modestly in place. Now that's a first. He
doesn't leave until the afternoon. We fill a leisurely morning
with sleep and getting-to-know-you conversations. He says
he doesn't want to leave – that he could stay in my bed
all day, and that he's planning on becoming a permanent

fixture if I'll have him. 'Maybe,' I tease, believing, without doubt, that I'll see him again.

He calls me the next night, as he said he would, to wish me sweet dreams. He follows this with regular texts throughout the week, and we make plans to meet up at the weekend. He seems reliable, and the right kind of keen that sidesteps needy, which is refreshing and very endearing.

Long story short, he came over last night. He called me at 10 p.m. after a night out with the lads, and I invited him over, for a late-night drink. His taxi pulled up fifteen minutes before midnight. 'A late-night drink.' Who was I kidding? Neither of us planned to roam North London looking for a late-night pub, something made clear by the fact that I answered the door in my pjs and bed socks. He's so broad and strong that I feel like a child in comparison, and when he sees me, he laughs and asks if I've been in that outfit since he left a week ago. Then he kisses me, lifts me as if I'm less than featherweight, and spins me around, saying he's missed me.

He said he didn't mind waiting. That he didn't expect anything, and that wasn't why he'd come. He'd be happy just to sleep next to me, he said earnestly – just to wake to see my beautiful face. But I wanted to please him. I wanted him to want me. I wanted him in me, because then he'd be close to me.

So I fucked him, three times, before he left at nine o'clock this morning. He promised to call me at lunchtime, but it's now almost midnight and my phone is silent, lying next to me on the arm of the sofa, mocking me. I know I won't hear from him again. A gut feeling? More likely I've just fucked enough men to read the signs. As I saw him out of the house he patted my arse and dodged away from my kiss. I'm just a conquest now, and no longer the girl he'll miss.

When midnight hits I call him, knowing he won't answer. He doesn't. I leave a cheery voicemail, asking him to call me back, and knowing that he won't. He doesn't. So I text him, with a masochistic urge to drive the last nail into the coffin. I know I shouldn't send that text, as it's a sure-fire way to make him run a further mile, but I need to know there's really no hope. Maybe he didn't hear his phone ring earlier, and now he assumes I'll be asleep so doesn't want to ring me? I'll just text and ask if he's got plans for tomorrow. He doesn't reply, and I get my answer. I turn my phone off and leave it that way until Sunday.

On Sunday I turn my phone back on, just as my mother, who has a sixth sense for when her daughter is in distress, phones.

'Something's wrong,' she says, before I've said more than good morning. It's not a question but a definite statement and, not for the first time, I wonder how she can read my mind so accurately from ten miles away.

'Amy, you forget, I carried you inside me,' she says, although I'm sure I didn't ask that question aloud. 'I can tell, even without speaking to you, when things aren't right or someone's upset you. What's happened? Is it something to do with Eoghan?'

I hate that. How my family assume it's always the dead husband: that all of my nerve endings lead to his coffin and I'm never upset by anything else.

'No,' I say defensively. 'It's not bloody Eoghan. I do have other problems too, you know.'

'So?' she asks, and waits. She has no doubt that I'll spill the beans eventually. I've always been a problem-shared sort of girl.

'It's the Australian,' I say, the last syllable of 'Australian' bleeding into tears. 'He hasn't called me back, and he promised me he would. He stayed here last night but now he's gone off me. He made so many promises, Mummy, and I was mug enough to believe them. Why do they do that?' I generalize. 'I can handle it if they're not interested, but I just hate all their bullshit and lies.'

'Did you have sex with him?' she asks. It may seem an odd question from a mother to her youngest daughter, but we, thankfully, don't have secrets in our family.

'No,' I answer. As soon as I hear the lie, I know that my conscience is far from clear. He hasn't called because I slept with him. The first, finite rule of dating, and the one I always seem to sidestep.

'Did you?' she interrogates.

'No!' My voice rises into an exclamation mark.

'Good,' she answers, 'because men never change, you know. They're simple creatures – ruled by their bollocks. And they're all after one thing, if they can get it.'

'I know, Mummy.' God, this is all I fucking need. 'But I didn't, OK, I'm not like that any more.' My chest feels tight. The raw nerve she's touched is tightening across my lungs. I'm going to cry.

'Why are you crying, Ame?' she asks. 'You didn't know him that well. There'll be plenty more men.'

'Because, because, you think I'm a whore,' I cry. 'And I promise, Mummy, I'm not any more. When Eoghan first died I slept with everyone, but I stopped all that. You know

I did. And now I've gone and let myself down, by letting a man get too close, too soon, again.'

'Enough, Amy,' she soothes, with the perfect mix of sympathy and sternness. She knows it's not good to encourage my self-pity. 'I do not think you're a whore. Far from it. But' – and this next bit is quite perfect – 'there're more intimate acts than sex, you know. And letting this man into your room, into your bed, and into your aura, leaves you just as vulnerable.'

I sniffle. She keeps talking. Saying things I'd never even considered, but that are instantly so obviously true to me.

'Ame, I know you inside out. You, and your sister, your personalities haven't really changed since you were babies. You were always the one who wanted cuddles – who always had her arms held out, looking to be picked up and held. You always needed to be touching someone – to have Daddy stroke your hair, or me rubbing your tummy. And when I watch you now, as an adult, you're still exactly the same. Out of both my daughters you're the one who wears her heart on her sleeve, and that's what makes you wonderful, but it's also your weakness. So, in a way, Ame, and I know this is a weird thing for a mother to say, it would be better for you to have sex with these men. Because letting them in your bed, to cuddle you, and nurture you, weakens your defences more than the sex does.'

This observation knocks me for six. I'd just never thought of the ramifications like that before.

I need to think more deeply about this, so I make an excuse to get off the phone. I call her back an hour later, and know she'll have been sitting by the home phone all

that time, waiting for me to get my thoughts straightened
and come back to her with my evaluation.

'I get lonely.'

'I know.'

'It's been nearly a year.'

'I know, darling girl.'

'You know, for a while after Eoghan died, I'd sleep with
anyone.'

'Yes' – there's not hint of surprise – 'you were fragile.'

'I just wanted to feel something. I wanted something to
take the edge off the emptiness. That's not enough for me
any more, but I don't remember how to act any differently. I can't remember the girl I was before Eoghan. I
don't know how to be that "normal" twenty-four-year-old.
So I'm stumbling around, making mistakes, chasing in-
appropriate men, and generally making a mess of things.'

'But Amy,' she laughs. 'Look around you. That's exactly
what twenty-four-year-olds do. Welcome back to the real
world, pet, you're as "normal" as the rest of them.'

I stop, and understand, and can't help laughing with her.

'But' – she stifles the laughter and her voice is stern
again – 'for someone so young, you have dealt with a lot:
Daddy's lymphoma, Eoghan dying. These are things that
would crack an adult, let alone a little girl.' I grimace at the
reference, but listen. 'I'm proud of you, Amy.' Her voice
cracks, and tears spring to the corners of my eyes. 'You've
overcome these things, and been so amazingly strong. But
I see the way you are with these men: so intense. Wanting
them in your bed the night you meet them, as if you want
it over and done with, knowing they'll dump you the next
day, and then you can happily hate them, and draw a line

through their name. Don't sabotage things before they've begun because you're scared of getting hurt again.'

That evening, lying in bed, mulling over the earlier conversation with my mother, I type out a lengthy text to Tyler. It's been a good while since we spoke, and I don't ever miss him, but I regret that we ended on such bad terms.

> Ty, please read on, because I just need to say this. I'm sorry for how I behaved when we were together. I was still hurting so badly from Eoghan dying and was looking for someone to lean on. I know I was needy and insecure and clung to you. I should have been more honest with you. All that filthy sex talk? That's not the real me. I just hid behind it because it was easier than being myself. Anyway, I've been thinking a lot and changing a lot recently. You got me at a tough point in my life and I'm sorry for causing you so much aggravation. I just wanted to say – that girl you knew – that's not the way I normally am, and not someone I'm proud to have been. But life sends you a bit topsy-turvy sometimes. Hopefully now I'm a lot nicer girl to have as a friend. It'd be good if we could be mates some day.

As the message sends, I realize I don't care if he replies. I feel lighter for just releasing the regrets.

He doesn't reply that night, but the next day, when my alarm goes off for work at 6.15, it's closely followed by a text from him.

'Are you awake?'

'Yep. Are you OK?'

'Sure. Just want you to listen to a song on YouTube I think you'll love.'

This was a game we played when we first started dating – before the drama and the problems and the quarrelling took over. We'd find new and obscure songs to match each other's character. Mine were always bubblegum pop. His were normally underground hip-hop.

The song's by Taio Cruz, an R&B singer. The title is 'She's like a Star', and I smile, knowing this is Tyler's olive branch.

Chapter Twelve

2 July 2008

I can't believe it's been a year. And what a year it's been. I've grown so much in that time. When I left Ireland, I promised myself I'd never look back. But now, one year on, there's no escaping my duties, and I'm strong enough to face them.

To commemorate Eoghan's one-year anniversary I have to fly back to Dublin for the first time since he died. There are things a widow is expected to do on these occasions: I must show my face at the memorial mass, visit the grave, etc., etc. There are traditions that need to be followed. None of them are particularly pleasant, but all of them are expected of me. My parents and I fly out of Heathrow on Sunday 29 June, spend two nights in the hotel where Eoghan and I married, then drive to Dublin City to visit his family. For weeks leading up to the trip I convince myself it won't affect me, that I've hardened enough to not let the memories reopen old wounds. But I underestimate the gripping power of Irish melancholy, and the days that follow very nearly kill me.

The evening before I fly, Rachel and I descend on Hoxton Square – a courtyard of bars where the talent is always exceptionally plentiful.

'A widow has to celebrate the first anniversary of her husband's death by having great sex with a stunningly beautiful stranger,' I say to Rachel levelly. 'I'm sure it's written in the bible somewhere or, if it isn't, I may write to the pope and ask him to add it to the New Testament.'

It's a marker of how well Rachel knows and accepts me that this comment doesn't even raise an eyebrow from her. She knows I threw out the 'How to Grieve' rulebook long ago, along with *Going It Alone, Living With Loss* and all the other self-help books my well-meaning relatives, and mostly my mother, posted to me – yes, posted: the cowards were too scared of my reaction to gift them face to face.

So, as I never shirk on a mission, sure enough, when I roll my suitcase out of the front door of my house at 6 a.m. the next morning, on my way to catch the tube to Heathrow airport, a bleary-eyed banker stumbles out behind me, knotting his tie back to front and gazing around to get his bearings. I kiss him goodbye at the front gate and nudge him in the direction of Highbury tube station. He mumbles something about meeting up for a date, so I punch my number into his mobile, whilst knowing full well I'll never see him again.

As the plane descends, through the blackening clouds, over Dublin, and grinds to a halt on the runway, I notice a hardened patch of come on my elbow. There wasn't enough time for a shower this morning, and I wonder if my mother, in the close-knit economy seat next to me, can smell the sex on me. If she can, I don't care. Because last night, I actually enjoyed myself. I fancied having sex, so I did, and that's the difference. I didn't do it to prove a point or as a form of therapy. I took him home because, like every twenty-something girl, sometimes I have an itch that needs scratching. It's simply all about balance. I don't need to choose all or nothing.

Waiting for the flight attendants to unlock the doors and release us into the arrivals lounge, I methodically flake the come off my elbow with my fingernail. It falls onto my lap and sits there like dandruff, but I don't shake it off. My mum glances down, but says nothing.

I gaze out the window and see the familiar skyline of Dublin in the distance. My stomach tightens and I'm thankful that last night I had the banker to distract me from this. For one sweaty hour, and a further twenty minutes for round two this morning, he took my mind off the fact that returning to Ireland was going to sting, more than I cared to admit.

The seatbelt lights above our heads dim, and the passengers seated around me clamber from their seats to grab their bags from the overhead lockers, elbowing each other in their haste to be the first in line through the passport check.

I'm in no rush, and my parents, waiting for my cue, sit equally still next to me. I shut my eyes and pray, for the first time in a long time: 'Please God, don't take me back to that place. I only just survived the first time round. I've mourned him enough; I don't have the energy to go through it again.' My mum reaches out for my hand and squeezes it tightly. I open my eyes and see that hers are shut tight.

A short time later, we've found our suitcases and collected

the hire car. It will take just over an hour to drive from the centre of Dublin to Aughrim, the small village in the county of Wicklow where Eoghan and I married, and where I and my parents will be staying for a 'therapeutic' weekend in the same hotel we had the wedding reception.

As we drive into the village, past the boulder-size stone 'Welcome' sign, the first thing I see is the church.

My parents see it too, and exchange worried glances – nobody is sure how I'm going to react – but I know what is expected of me so, 'Let's stop,' I say. 'We should light a candle for him whilst we're here. His mum would like us to anyway.'

The grounds of the church seem bigger and darker without our wedding guests cheering up the tombstones. As I climb the steps of the church porch, I can't help but think of the last time I was here, walking out in the opposite direction: leaving the church a fresh new bride, hand in hand with my husband, neither of us quite believing how lucky we were to have made it that far.

Today, as I heave open the oak doors of the church, my parents are just one step behind me. I know they think they're a welcome support, but oh God, I wish I was alone. I can sense them both holding their breath right now, waiting: Is she going to cry, is she going to scream, is she going to fall apart again?

It unnerves me more that I don't want to do any of these things. My emotions are totally even. I stand at the entrance to the church and survey the building, waiting for the emotional tidal wave to hit.

But this isn't the church where I married. This church is empty. How can it upset me? The church where I married was full of love, laughter and hope: friends, family and masses of springtime flowers. Today, my footsteps echo off the walls as I walk up the aisle. Without my husband there, standing at the altar, I don't recognize this place and have no reason for being here. 'Let's go,' I tell my parents, and walk back out, feeling nothing but alone.

The staff of the Brooklodge Hotel, where our wedding reception was held, always treated Eoghan and I like royalty. We first came here on Eoghan's thirty-sixth birthday, the May before he died. His friends paid for the trip. They sensed we needed a break, and we found the hotel to be such a haven of serenity, tucked away in the Irish country-side, that we returned regularly after that, to escape from the city after particularly tough bouts of treatment.

In this time, Eoghan, with his indiscriminate charm, left quite an impression on the hearts of the staff, and every person I meet has a story to recount about my husband. Now, I know I should be more generous, as these people are praising him with the best of intentions, but all this adoration soon gets on my nerves. I don't need to be told my husband is wonderful. I know! Jesus, I am the one that married him. It might be nice to hear these things if he were still alive and with me, when I could hang off his arm, proud and smug that he is mine. But must I remind them that he's gone? He's dead, and we're a whole year on. Indeed, praising him to the rooftops only reminds me of what I've lost.

Unfortunately, it seems, because of the forthcoming anniversary, Eoghan is the hot topic of the day, and every conversation I have through the weekend is spot-lit on him.

My mother is happy to talk for hours about him, but I spend a lot of time sat in silence, with these conversations circling around my head.

On Sunday evening we are joined by Eoghan's brother and his girlfriend and one of Eoghan's closest friends, Sean. His mother has decided not to join us – just one year on she finds it too hard to come back here – and I am beginning to agree with her.

That said, it is nice to see Eoghan's friends and family again. I was worried about facing them, having avoided their phone calls and letters for so long, but now find I'm genuinely pleased to see them. I apologize for not keeping in touch, but they bat my sorrys away with the backs of their hands and say they completely understand.

We settle ourselves in the hotel bar. I sit with my mother on my left-hand side and a knee-high sculpture of an elephant on my right. Did I tell you this was Eoghan's favourite animal? The contradiction between their strength and grace appealed to him. We had elephant models, in varying guises, dotted around our house in Dalkey. I didn't particularly like them – mainly because I had to clean them – but I did bury Eoghan with the smallest one – a carved oak model with one tusk missing that was no bigger than the palm of his hand. I buried Eoghan with quite a haul in the end. The undertakers must have thought I was mad – but then I'm sure they've had stranger requests.

I nestle into the quilted cushions of the sofa, drape my right hand over the armrest and let my palm rest on the elephant's head. I idly stroke a curve of metal that runs from the trunk and into a tusk and let the small talk around me wash over me. The conversation is unthreatening, and revolves around the weather forecast, sports results and the latest fall in interest rates. I'm in comfortable territory.

Then the exchange takes an all too familiar path: a well-worn topic that will become the order of the weekend. Namely, 'How often we think about, talk about or miss Mr Eoghan Molloy, the deceased.'

'I talk to him every day,' Sean says. 'If I have any worries or problems, I only have to ask old Eoghan's advice and things always turn out right.'

'I'm forever chatting to him,' my mother joins in. 'Most nights, when I'm lying in bed, or even when I'm just sitting at my desk at work, I chat, chat, and chat away to him. Also, do you know, since the funeral I find white feathers everywhere I go – and that's supposed to be a sign that an angel is close by.'

'I cried just yesterday, thinking about him,' says Marian, the girlfriend of Eoghan's older brother, Fergus. 'I was driving home from work when a song came on the radio – that *Moulin Rouge* number that was the first dance at the wedding – and the tears started flowing. I had to pull over to the side of the road because I was in such a state.'

My mother, not wanting to be outdone, pipes up on my father's behalf: 'Well, Steve will tell you, he doesn't go a day without talking with Eoghan.'

I glance at my dad, but he shrugs apologetically then nods in agreement. Traitor, I think. My mother's still going: 'Steve will be out in the back garden, filling up the bird-feeders, and I know he's talking to Eoghan, because I can see his lips moving.'

'I just ask that he watches over Amy and helps her,' interrupts my father.

All eyes swivel to me at the mention of my name, and stay there. Apparently it's my turn to share. I lick my lips, hoping it might lubricate some conversation, but what can I say? I'm the only one who doesn't talk to my husband.

OK, that's not strictly true. I do toss the odd comment Eoghan's way, but I don't spend my days conversing with him in great depth, swapping stories and asking him for advice. I have flesh-and-blood friends for that, who are far more vocal in their feedback.

Will I be struck down if I admit that now, on an average day, I don't even miss him?

How can these people still spend so much time pining? I have to hold down a full-time job – if I still dedicated that many hours to missing him, I'd never get any work done. It's one year on and, though mourning Eoghan was once my priority, I had to draw that to a close because I had a life to lead.

'Isn't it time to start letting go?'

I don't say this out loud but I want to.

Eoghan would sock it to them straight, of course – he had no time or patience for people feeling sorry for themselves, but I know it's not my place to say. And I know it's not an easy thing to do.

It's taken every ounce of my strength to move on, but I did. I built a new life because I had no other choice. It might not be a perfect life, and not all my choices are commendable, but at least I'm moving forward, taking baby steps in stilettos, as I couldn't bear to be still *there*.

'I, I . . .' I'm at a loss for words.

In London I can speak freely and I know my friends

will never judge me, but I'm back in Ireland now, and here I know my place.

'Well, you know, I have my ups and downs. I still cry every day,' the widow says.

The lie blisters my mouth with its acidity. I go to bed shortly after that, with my stomach in knots. I'm utterly disappointed in myself for conforming.

The next day we plant a tree in the hotel grounds in celebration of Eoghan's life. It was my mother's idea that my father then put into action, liaising with Evan, the hotel's owner, and Gregg, the hotel's gardener, both of whom join us for the planting.

I adore Evan. He's one of those mystical men whose age is impossible to distinguish because they exude youth. I've always loved Evan, from the first time I met him, when we came to the hotel for that weekend break on Eoghan's thirty-sixth birthday. I had pre-warned the hotel about Eoghan's condition – just covering our backs in case things took a downturn – and Evan had gone out of his way to accommodate us, even upgrading our room to a mezzanine suite free of charge so we would have a fridge to store Eoghan's medicines. He was there to greet us when we arrived, on our final night joined us for a glass of red wine and, somewhere in between this, Eoghan and he sealed a friendship.

It was not unusual, in the run-up to our wedding, for me to wake at midnight, or even three in the morning, to find the pillow next to me empty, the bedroom door ajar, and hear Eoghan chatting away to someone on the phone.

'Who were you talking to?' I'd ask, when forty minutes later my fiancé would tiptoe back to bed.

'Just Evan,' was the stock reply.

'What were you talking about at this time of night?'

'I was asking his opinion on my suit for the wedding.'

Or: 'We were talking about the best place to surf in Ireland.'

Or simply: 'I was just telling him about a dream I had.'

At the funeral it would be Evan who'd hug me the hardest and whisper in my ear: 'It was an honour to know him.'

Today, he leads our small group across the hotel gardens to a small plot of earth already turned over in preparation. The weather couldn't possibly be more dreadful. A severe-weather warning had been issued that morning and the wind was so fierce the rain seemed to fall horizontally in its force.

We must make an odd sight, standing outside in the storm's eye, assembled around a hole in the ground. It's no wonder the other guests peer out of the hotel windows, trading theories about what we could possibly be doing.

My father had asked the hotel gardener to choose a fitting tree: one that would represent Eoghan's larger-than-life personality but also suit the garden's soil type. After much research on his part, Gregg picked a Handkerchief tree, which he promises will grow to a hulking size and blossom around our wedding anniversary each year.

It is the perfect tribute to Eoghan, who loved the great outdoors and was never happier than when he was stripped to the waist, walking barefoot across a grassy field, over-grown woodland, or stretch of unspoilt beach.

Evan hands the spade to Fergus, who turns the earth methodically before lifting the tree and gingerly placing it into the pit.

My mother sniffs. Sean wipes his nose on the back of his hand. She passes him a crumpled tissue from her pocket, followed by one for Marian and then two for herself.

I watch the stump of a tree being placed in the ground and think, What is all the fuss about?

This changes as Evans carries the plaque from the hotel and lays it at the base of the tree. I chose the words myself, five weeks before, when my father asked if I had a preference as to what was written, but seeing them now, carved into a thick block of cedar wood, makes them so much more poignant.

Eoghan Molloy. 2 July 2007.
Free as a Bird, Safe with the Angels.

My tears match the rain, droplet for droplet. My mother and father gravitate towards me, but it is Evan who reaches me first and gathers me into his arms. I press my cheek into the creases of his coat as he bends to press his lips against the crown of my head, my hair now sodden and matted with rain.

It is the first time since Eoghan died that I have been held like this without the undertone of sex, and the affection in this simple gesture penetrates my armour. I close my eyes, loosen my muscles and let Evan take my bodyweight. My shoulders heave and my gentle tears turn into wailing sobs.

'I know,' Evan murmurs into my ear, 'I know, I know, I know.' His own voice breaks on the fourth repetition, and his tears run down the side of my neck, gathering in the hollow of my collarbone.

'He loved you, you know,' I say into his chest, hoping I haven't chosen too intimidating a word.

'The feeling was mutual.'

I push away from his chest and angle my face up to his. His eyes are chestnut brown but match Eoghan's in their kindness, which is a rare and precious thing.

'Thank you, Evan. For all this. You've really done him proud.'

I stand on tiptoes to kiss his cheek.

'And for the wedding . . . I never thanked you.'

'Hush now.' His lip bottom lip trembles. 'I was just thankful to know him.'

I cast my eyes to the river that borders the garden, to the spot where we had our wedding photographs taken, but my view is blocked by an unbroken sheet of rain.

'He enjoyed the day, didn't he, Evan?' I ask softly. 'Do you think he was happy to marry me?'

'Amy' – the sharpness of his tone is unusual – 'I don't know how on earth you can question that.'

'I don't know. I just do. I don't trust my own memories. And on our wedding night we had a huge barney . . .' It's the first time I've confessed that to anyone but my parents.

'Amy' – he cups my chin and raises it, so I'm forced to meet his eye line – 'I watch a lot of weddings in this place. But I've never, ever, seen a groom look so happy. You ask anyone who works here.'

'But that night, after the reception . . .'

'I also talked to Eoghan the morning after your wedding. He came to thank me – you were away in the swimming pool. And do you know what he said to me? He said he couldn't understand how he'd got so lucky.'

My jaw drops.

'I know, Amy, that you probably don't believe me.'

'No, I do. I just realized he said exactly the same thing to me.'

Like a slide dropping into a carousel projector, an image appears in my head: Eoghan and me, on the first afternoon of our honeymoon, in the hotel spa's jacuzzi.

I'm seated on Eoghan's lap, laughing as the bubble jets inflate his shorts around my waist. He has his hands rested behind his head, eyes half closed and a contented smile on his face.

'I love my wife,' he says.

'I love my husband more.'

He shifts his weight, wraps his arms around my waist and sticks his index finger in my belly button, causing me to shriek and wiggle.

'But, seriously, Amox,' he says when I'm resettled, 'tell me how I got this lucky.'

I raise an eyebrow, not sure if he's for real.

'I mean it. I never thought I'd meet a girl like you. Let alone marry her. I've got everything I ever dreamed of right here. I couldn't ask for anything more.'

Eoghan's face fades to Evan's, and I ask him: 'Why couldn't I remember that before?'

'Because sometimes it's more painful to draw to mind the good times.'

As he says this, a wave of sadness washes over me: 'Fuck, I miss him so much.'

And although it passes as quickly as it comes, it leaves me shaken and unnerved.

I grip Evan's hand even tighter, searching for stability,

but he kisses my cheek and pulls firmly away, saying: 'I'm going to leave you to it now. But come and say goodbye before you go.'

I wipe my eyes on the hankerchief he's slipped into my hand, run my fingers through my hair and re-knot my scarf so the fringed edges are perfectly in line.

My dad moves to hug me, but I brush him away with a signature 'I'm fine'.

But something's changed, and I'm not. I can't convince myself this time. Something around me has shifted and, as I walk back to the hotel, I'm not as sure-footed as I was when I walked out.

After settling the bill, it's time to drive back to Dublin. The next stop on our journey is the Molloy family home, where each of the five brothers were born and raised. Eoghan and I also lived there for two months when he was originally diagnosed, so the house is brimming with mixed memories.

When we arrive at number 73 I don't ring the doorbell but instead reach for the key that's trustingly left under the mat. The key jars in the lock, as it always has, and as usual I think, 'That needs oiling.' Here, no time has passed, yet for me so much is different.

Eoghan's mother appears from the kitchen as I walk down the hallway. She looks older than I remember, but then what else can I expect after the year that's behind her? He was the second son Pauline had lost – Eoghan's older brother Edmund drowned in his twenties – so I can't even imagine the effect of such a double blow.

Pauline greets me with outstretched arms and I'm awash with affection for my mother-in-law: such a strong and dignified woman. Eoghan used to say we were one and the same. I realize I've missed her as well as her son.

As my parents and Pauline settle in the living room, I offer to make a pot of tea and escape to the kitchen. Whilst waiting for the kettle to boil, my gaze strays to the staircase. There's no use avoiding it. The only bathroom in the house is on the second floor so, unless I don't drink anything for the rest of the evening, I'm going to have to pass our bedroom at some point. Best to face it: to rip off the Band-Aid.

The room has been recently redecorated. The curtains are new, and our old double bed has been replaced by two singles. But it's not like I care about the furnishings, just as long as the walls haven't been repainted. Because I've come in here to check one thing.

And there it is, gouged in chalk across the chimneybreast wall: 'I love you, Eogh. No doubts.' I had written it one tempestuous day in December after we'd had a blazing row. About what? I don't know, I can't even remember now.

Our arguments back then were fleeting. We'd both lash out, angrier at the cancer than each other, but we'd have kissed and made up before our shouts turned into echoes.

'I love you, Eogh. No doubts.'

It makes me smile even now, seeing those words on the wall, smudged around the edges but still easily legible. Those words became our motto. Whatever trial was thrown at us, we believed doubtlessly that our love could overcome it. We believed we'd be just fine as long as we had each other. I can smile even now because it was so true: I never had any doubts; I always knew he was it for me, I knew he was all I'd ever need.

'You bastard,' I say. 'You were easier to hate.'

To still love him so infinitely – that's a whole lot harder.

'How long does it take to boil a kettle?' my father hollers from the living room.

'Sorry. Just coming,' I call.

Eoghan's favourite mug is still there, sitting right at the back of the kitchen cabinet and, as it's mottled with dust, I suspect nobody has drunk from it since he last did. Is it impolite for me to use it? I decide that, as his wife, I have rights, so run it under the tap and add it to the tea tray with the others.

As I walk into the living room and place the tea tray on the table Pauline raises an eyebrow that says, 'Duly noted,' but there's also a smile that lets me know she permits it.

For the next five hours a steady stream of neighbours and well-wishers rotate through Pauline's living room. Although their interest is well meaning, by the fifteenth visitor I begin to feel like a circus act: 'Roll up, roll up! Come and see the twenty-four-year-old widow. See how she's grown, just one year on!'

Each person asks how I'm getting on in London and, out of perfunctory courtesy, I tell them the basics about my house and my job. However, when they push me for anecdotes, I clam up.

Where do I start? What can I tell them? Every story I want to share needs to be censored. Should I tell the local reverend about my otherwise-engaged lover? Or maybe I should start with last week's banker, whose name by this stage I can't even remember. I can't tell them about my house-mates and our single-girl antics, or about the stream of men I bring home at night and kick out before breakfast.

I decide the safe option is silence, so spend the last hour raising Eoghan's mug to my lips and shrugging every time someone asks me a question. The lady who runs the corner shop looks at me, turns to the postman and whispers, 'She's broken, poor pet, life must be quite unbearable.'

I hope that if I stay still and quiet long enough, I might disappear altogether.

I wake the next morning, thankful that it's our last day in Dublin. Eoghan's memorial mass is scheduled for 10 a.m., so I focus on midday, when all this will be over.

However, when we arrive at the church at 9.25 – 'to get the best seats' – Pauline tells us that, because a local pensioner died two days before, Eoghan's mass will be combined with her funeral.

This slight glitch doesn't deter our party. As Pauline says: 'A mass is a mass after all.' So we follow in the path of the funeral procession, even though none of us knows the poor lady's name.

I'm shunted into a ringside pew, right next to the coffin, in a somewhat unsympathetic seating arrangement. But I don't have the energy to move or protest: by this stage in our trip I'm emotionally exhausted and so used to keeping schtum I think my lips have sealed together.

The old lady's grandson stands to do the first reading. Not the brightest bulb in the box, he stutters through the words with a thick Dublin accent and I feel a giggle tremble in the pit of my stomach. It rises up my oesophagus and, though I try to hold it down, my chest starts to vibrate with the palpitations of the raucous laughter I can feel brewing.

The grandson, hampered by nerves, has developed a lisp by the last verse of the reading, and stutters five times on the final 'salvation'. I dig my fingers into my palms as he draws to a halt, closing his prayerbook and stepping down from the altar. Thank God, I think. And then he trips.

His left foot gets caught on the gold tassels of the cloth covering the altar, and he puts his arms out just quickly enough to save himself. Not a spectacular fall, but enough to push me over the edge.

I snort through my nostrils, in a very unladylike fashion. And then I snicker, though I manage to muffle the noise in my tissue. Still, every mourner in the pew ahead turns to glare at me, and then in domino fashion the row in front catches on and turn to glare as well.

Eoghan would find this hilarious, I think. He was always one for laughing at the most inconvenient moments. He once got a fit of the giggles in hospital as the nurse was trying to administer an enema, and laughed so hard it popped right back out. So you can see why he'd appreciate this moment.

'Eoghan,' I mumble into my saliva-soaked tissue, 'you god-awful git, you're not making this easy for me, are you?'

I wipe my eyes and rearrange my expression into one of grief. Thankfully, those in the congregation recognize me and, with nudges of 'widow', they interpret my chuckling as tears.

They're not the only ones who are confused. I can barely keep up with my emotions this week. I don't know whether I'm coming or going.

* * *

Soon after the mass is over, it's time for us to drive to the airport and catch our night flight home to Heathrow. Though I'm happy to be leaving, I still find it hard saying goodbye to Pauline. I wish I could do more to help her and feel guilty that I don't see her more often. I know that, unless a special occasion unfolds, I won't be back now for at least another year. Although I loudly promise I'll be back soon, I know, and she knows, it isn't true.

I say hasty goodbyes and then go and wait in the car for my parents. Dublin's due for a storm, and the air is muggy, so I open the window to let in a waft of breeze. My mum and Eoghan's are standing a few feet from the car, and I catch the tail end of their conversation.

'From the first day he met her,' Pauline is saying, 'all he talked about was Amy. It was Amy this and Amy that. I never had any doubts about those two, Eoghan was as in love as any man could be and you could see she was the same. It's just so heartbreaking. How could any God do that to a girl so young?'

'I know,' my mother agrees. 'You just had to see them together. Love like that is so rare these days.'

I grab at the handle for the window, hastily rolling it up and muting the conversation in mid-flow. I feel sick. Sick and tired of being seen as a victim. Sick of my husband for being painted as a saint.

I'm fiercely angry at my husband. For fuck's sake, Eoghan, why have you put me in this situation? I shouldn't be doing this. I shouldn't be a fucking widow. This isn't how life's meant to turn out. I just want to feel what it's like to be normal.

For the first time in a long time I'm not in control, and

this scares me. There's no logic to my thoughts, and that isn't like me. Involuntarily, I start to shake. What if this is it? What if I get sucked back to square one again?

When I came back to England in the aftermath of Eoghan's death, there's no denying I was a mess. Without Eoghan, I had no interest in living and no motivation to keep going. I couldn't walk. I couldn't talk. I couldn't even brush my teeth unsupervised. My nerve endings were numb, cut off with a tourniquet of grief. I was paralysed. I'd pinch my arm until I bled and still feel nothing. My senses were completely dead. And the tiredness was all-consuming. Most mornings my mum would lift me out of bed and dress me. Walking the length of the house was a marathon. I was a walking corpse – locked and bound in the coffin with him. And let me tell you, it took all my strength to claw my way out again. I worked too damn hard to keep tabs on my grief to now, one year on, let it get the better of me.

I hear him clearly now, his voice strong and unmistakable, repeating the words I said on his deathbed.

'You can go now, Amy. You haven't let me down. You did everything you could. You did everything you promised me you would. You can go now, Amy.'

I look down at my left hand. It's been fisted for a year, my fingers wrapped tightly around an imaginary hand: terrified to let go of him, petrified to go on alone.

I place the flat of my palm to my lips and kiss it softly.

'You're right, Eoghs, it's time to go now,' I agree.

I uncurl my fingers and pull my hand from his. I know he'll always be near me, but don't want him quite so close, nor holding me quite so tight. 'Goodbye, my baby.'

On the plane journey home, I drown out my thoughts with my iPod. It belonged to Eoghan actually – it's the same one he was wearing when he died – although I have changed the earphones since then. His music is still stored on here, although I haven't listened to most of the songs. Let's just say my husband and I had very different tastes – with a thirteen-year age gap, we were from different musical generations. But today, bored with my choices, I scan through his playlists, and see one marked 'For A'.

'For A.' No, it can't be. My mind's playing tricks on me. But, intrigued, I click into it, and find there's only one song listed.

The one single song in the playlist is 'You Could be Happy' by Snow Patrol. I don't recognize the song, and I'd never known Eoghan to mention it, but my instincts say I'm not wrong. 'For A' is 'For Amy'.

PLAY.

As the song begins, my jaw drops. The words are so fitting they could have been written for me, and the sentiments so typically Eoghan that it's like he's standing there speaking to me.

'You can be happy,' he tells me. 'And I hope you are.

'You made me happier than I'd been by far.

'Do the things that you always wanted to. Without me there to hold you back, don't think, Ame, just do. Take a glorious bite out of the whole world.'

I press repeat for the fifth time as the plane descends into Heathrow. My hands have stopped shaking but my tears are still falling, calmly, however, in pearly droplets. The skin on my arms is raised in goosebumps. And my heart has swelled with such a cocktail of pure joy and sorrow that it doesn't know whether to burst or collapse.

I see now he has been there at every junction in my year. As I've fumbled and tumbled with many different men, chased after the bad guys and pushed away the good, he never deserted me, but just took a back seat. He was there the night I found out my new boyfriend was engaged. The morning I woke up black and blue, with a Dear John note propped beside my bed. He was there when I cried with loneliness and when I'd prayed for a sign he was still in my life. Even when I was sure I'd shooed him away, and had left my past behind me. He was there all along: dormant but waiting, for when I was ready to connect with him again.

By the time I get back to Islington it's 2 a.m. The sky is quite starless. I look left and right and see, corner to corner, only dark angry cloud cover. My parents drop me outside the house. We've been through so much I don't even need to explain how I feel.

My mum walks me from the car to the doorstep.

'This really isn't necessary,' I tell her. 'I think I can find my own way up the garden path.'

'I know, but I wanted a word with you before you went in,' she says, cupping my face. 'I know you better than anyone else in the world. And I know this week was harder for you than you had imagined, but darling, we all knew it wasn't going to be easy. You might be strong, but you're not invincible. And it was only a year ago that you buried your husband.'

'Exactly, Mummy, it was a year ago. How can I still be upset about this?'

'Oh, for God's sake, Amy, cut yourself some slack.'

There's that saying again. Jesus, did Eoghan rehearse this with everybody?

'Finding this trip hard was not a sign of weakness. Darling, you're only human. The problem is you've come so far that, looking back, you can't quite see the length of the distance you've travelled.'

'Have I though, Mummy? Or am I kidding myself? When we were back in Dublin, I felt like I was back at square one.'

'I know. It was hard for all of us. But those feelings will pass. Amy, they will,' she repeats, dragging out the vowel in my name. 'You're back home now, and you'll feel yourself again. Take from this trip the realization that you made the right choice moving home from Ireland. Here, with the girls, you've found a place where you can be, and achieve, anything and not be pigeonholed into what other people think you should be.'

'But what sort of a widow am I?' I challenge.

'You're the best kind' – my mother hugs me tightly – 'and don't let anyone tell you any different. You're a survivor, Amy. You dig in your heels and do anything you must to get by. And that's exactly what Eoghan loved about you, remember that.'

I close the front door behind me, leave my suitcase in the hallway and trip tiredly into my bedroom, relieved to be home.

That night I sleep alone. With no lover. And no husband. I starfish across the mattress, stretching my fingers and toes to the bedposts. And the freedom I once found so lonely and so fearsome is actually, wonderfully, liberating.